Shlomo Kalo
*FOREVERMORE*

All Rights Reserved to
Y  D.A.T.  PUBLICATIONS
P.O.Box 27019
Jaffa 61270 Israel
dat@y-dat.co.il,
www.y-dat.co.il
Phone: +972-3-5071239

ISBN: 978-965-7028-64-3

Original Hebrew edition: *"Ad Olam"* by DAT
Publications, Jaffa, Israel.
Published in Romanian by Editoura Hasefer,
Bucharest.

English Translation by Michael (Martin) S. Howard
and Jerry Aviram.
Edited by Richard Flantz.

Cover Design: Pradeep. Based on a photo taken by
Albert Cusian in 1941, Warsaw Ghetto.
Permission by Bundesarchiv.

Shlomo Kalo

# FOREVERMORE

# Table of Contents

Some Introductory Remarks

Zabir Ben Bata................................................9

The Garden of the Saint Janusz........55

Ivan Novotny...............................................115

# Some Introductory Remarks

Different peoples and nations in the world are noted for their unique attributes, annals and exploits. And not a few have passed from the stage of history, leaving behind nothing but ruins and legends.

The people of Israel and the Jewish nation, too, have a singular attribute of their own that sets them completely apart from all other peoples and languages: the Jews have retained, exclusively for themselves, nine of the ten measures of pain and suffering given to the world.

The people of Israel is hated by all peoples and nations, but most of all – by themselves.

The inevitable question is: Why?

There are those who would not dare ask this question, while others avoid it or pretend that it does not exist, and still others who declare unequivocally that it has no answer. Nonetheless, there have been those who, upright and pure of heart, not only publicly posed the question in all its acuteness, but also strove to answer it.

One of those exceptional individuals was Rabbi Shlomo Virga, who was born in Malaga in Spain and lived in the fifteenth century. In his book *The Tribe of Judah* he articulated this gnawing question as follows:

"Why this great anger?"

Good scholar that he is, he lists the reasons, one after the other:

"One - the sins of our forefathers...; two – ...because of hatred of religion and the ruler's love of subjugating human beings to his own religion and faith, as was said by our Sages of blessed memory: 'Why is its name Sinai? Because hatred *(sin'a)* descended from it...' When our religion proscribes eating and drinking with others, which brings people closer together, as was said by our Sages: 'Great is the sipping that brings closer those who are far apart'...; three - the killing of Jesus of Nazareth...; four - because the three great jealousies are: religious jealousy, jealousy of women, jealousy of wealth, and all these exist among Israel...; five - because the Jewish people have become accustomed to bearing false witness...; and six - the pride with which a few of our people have sought to rule over the Gentiles..."

*Forevermore* deals with real events and people from the past, and attempts to describe the Jew as he is and not as he is perceived, against the backdrop of the historical facts and the spirit of the period and the era.

# ZABIR BEN BATA

ZAHR DER RAJA

## The Desert

Our story begins in the desert, where it will also end. This desert is today within the borders of the Kingdom of Saudi Arabia. In those far-off days, there existed many kingdoms, in a profusion and diversity hitherto unknown, and not a single one of these laid claim to so vast a sea of sand and crumbling rock, nor did it ever occur to any king or ruler to demand sovereignty over it. It was a no-man's-land designed by nature for its own reasons, and was respected by men who dared not provoke it or rise against it.

## A Road

From time immemorial, the desert was a road. A road linking east to west, north to south, one sea to another sea, one remote and flourishing kingdom to another distant and no less flourishing one. Camel caravans traversed it, laden with choice silks, perfumes and spices, myrrh and frankincense, silver, porcelain, gold, and a variety of goods, and returned with the proceeds secured in the money belts of the brave merchants and in tiny padlocked cedar chests. At times, much too frequently, the merchants paid dearly for their dreams of power and glory, riches and luxuries, with the robbers benefiting at their expense. The corpses of the dreamers tumbled beneath the hoofs of their trembling beasts and were mercifully covered by the hot sands.

## The Oasis

The oasis is the very heart of the wasteland, proof that it lives and that life can adapt to it despite its severe nature which strikes all who behold it with awe, fills their hearts with a sense of inadequacy, and engenders wonderment. Those who manage to adapt to the desert's monotonous vistas, its fearfully majestic silence that encompasses a lethal power, can be divided into two groups: robbers and thinkers. Both strive single-mindedly toward one goal: to be masters of the world, claiming passionately that this is their destiny. History has proven that their claims are not without foundation.

## Mecca

It so happened that, with the passage of time, an oasis became transformed from a temporary resting place into a permanent settlement, and eventually into a city. Before long, the city became a "state", that is, it was encompassed by a wall which imparted an intoxicating sense of power, pride and security to its residents, igniting in their hearts an uncompromising striving for dominion, conquests and luxuries.

Mecca passed through all the stages of this process: from a desert oasis, to a temporary encampment, a permanent settlement, a city, and eventually – a "state". In its early days, when it was an oasis, it was visited by wandering Yemenite tribes, and later on the Romans and then the Byzantines found it to be of some interest. Ultimately, the Ishmaelite tribes, known today as the Bedouin Arabs, emerged from the desert and settled there in their multitudes, and founded parties which to this very day continue to operate according to a tribal key. When the time was ripe and demand became great, the residents of Mecca discovered that the ancient structure standing in its center was none other than the building erected by Abraham with his son Ishmael, born to him of his wife's handmaiden, Hagar the Egyptian. The Meccans of that time viewed the structure as a sort of temple of God, and began to worship it, installing within it their images and statues, mystical symbols, and other clear symbols of what is perceived as idolatry by the monotheistic religions.

### The Expectation

It was impossible for this situation to continue, with each tribe, clan and family installing its own private image within the holy structure of Abraham and Ishmael and worshipping it, fervently, it is true, but each in its own way, contradictory to that of its neighbor, each group claiming its own image to be supreme over all others and, to prove its claim, going to war against those who claimed otherwise. It was inevitable that a man should appear who would call the Meccans to order and put an end to the bloodshed, and decide which among the images was the most powerful, imparting comfort, wealth and assured victory to its worshippers. And should the warlike tribal chiefs find this decision unacceptable, then he would install a new image, his own, or in extremity would remove all the images and announce some revolutionary innovation, which would unite the fractured Arab nation and secure its place among the nations and its validity as the bearer of a vision and harbinger of good tidings and innovations.

What was needed, then, was a message, and even more, a bearer of the message, or better still, a bearer of a prophecy or, simply, a prophet who was an Arab.

## Muhammad

In the year 570 C.E., a son was born to Abd-Allah, or Abdallah, the son of Abd Al-Muttalib (Abd-Allah Ibn Abd Al-Muttalib) of the Hashemite tribe, at the time considered to be a fruitful and thriving family, and today a tribal party which rules a number of Islamic states. He was given the name "Muhammad". If we trace the name back to its ancient Hebrew root, it would appear that the newborn child aroused joy and affection in those around him, and they named him "Hammud" (lovable) or "Mahmad" (darling).

It appears that fate, which the Ishmaelite tribes of those days respected, in contrast to the present times, when they believe in it with unrestrained fervor, was not kind to the infant Muhammad. His father, that same Abd-Allah Ibn Abd Al-Muttalib, died before the birth of the "darling", and his son never set eyes on him.

The grandfather, Abd Al-Muttalib, who held a place of honor in the hierarchy of the Meccan

Hashemite tribe, undertook responsibility for raising the infant.

Heeding the advice of medical experts and of men who were wise in all matters, who said that the air of Mecca was unhealthy for his grandson, he delivered the child into the care of a friendly desert tribe, where a wet nurse was found for him.

The crisp air of the wilderness, its isolating silence, its spaces that conceal secrets, the breathtaking majestic sunrises and fiery sunsets that light up the entire horizon, were the sights that the child saw and the air that he breathed and absorbed.

At the age of six, Muhammad was orphaned of his mother Aminah of the Zuhra clan, and two years later his grandfather joined Muhammad's parents in death.

Muhammad was taken to live with his uncle, Abu Talib, who at the time was chief of the Hashemites. The boy, accompanying him with the camel caravans to Syria and back, encountered new faces, different peoples and foreign tribes, and learned the intricacies of trade while supporting himself honorably as bodyguard to the wealthy merchants who accompanied his uncle on his trips. On one of these trips, around the year 595, he served as aide and guardsman to a wealthy and respected lady in her forties, Khadigah of the exalted House of Assad, who fell desperately in love with him and offered him marriage, conclusive evidence that Muhammad had lost none of his charm, which elicited from others affection, admiration and, apparently, love as well.

Muhammad consented to Khadigah, out of considerations which, notwithstanding the many studies and logical conclusions on the subject, remain beclouded to this very day, and will likely never be revealed and known until the end of days. One way or another, regardless of his indisputable right and the wealth which he obtained upon his marriage, Muhammad did not take another wife besides Khadigah, until her death in the year 619 C.E. She bore him two sons, who died one after the other, and four daughters, the best known of whom was Fatimah, who married Ali, Muhammad's cousin, his future heir and founder of the Shi'ite branch of Islam. Muslims see fate's guiding hand in the marriage of their prophet to Khadigah, since without Khadigah's riches Muhammad would not have had the time to conceive his plans, nor the means to realize them.

## The Revelation

Even before he got married, Muhammad was wont to go off alone to find brief spates of solitude in one of the desert caves in the vicinity of Mecca. He continued this practice even after his marriage, and it must be said to his wife's credit that not only did she not object or try to dissuade him, but she treated his strange behavior with respect, and in some ways even encouraged him. During one of these retreats, probably in the year 610, a radiant figure appeared to Muhammad and, as he related, addressed him, telling him that he had been chosen to be the messenger of God. Later, Muhammad defined and named the figure as the angel Gabriel.

Muhammad had no further revelations but, as he testified, he heard God's voice within himself, and he transmitted what he heard.

His wife's cousin, Waragah the Christian, was the first interpreter of the revelation. He firmly asserted that Muhammad had been called to take a place of honor among the holy messengers and ancient prophets of the Bible, to bring the word of God to his people and set them upon the path to redemption. This interpretation was accepted with satisfaction and without any hesitation or reservation, and was adopted at once, quite literally.

## A New Religion

Rumors of the revelation and the gospel spread among the hut-dwellers of Mecca, even reaching its nobility, the residents of the castles and palaces, but impressed no one. It could be reasonably assumed that the whole matter would have been forgotten and erased from memory while still in its inception, had it not been for Muhammad's stubborn persistence and his dedication, noteworthy from any standpoint, to what according to Waragah was his destiny.

Muhammad began to preach. He would speak to anyone who would listen to him and instill in his listener's heart a clear and simple religion, which he called "Islam" – "Submission", meaning sincere and total submission to the almighty God, who is the one and only true God. He called his "submitting" believers "Muslims", the chosen among humans, who strive with all their hearts to carry out God's will; and who do so in practice. Through His Prophet, this God warns humans, who were created in His image, not to stray in the ways of chaos, not to sin, and not to covet the well-being of others. And above all, they are to avoid pride as they would a consuming fire. And when the godly human soul departs the sinful fleshly body to stand judgment before the Lord of all the worlds, He will judge it by its actions and behavior on earth: to cast it down to anguish in Hell or raise it to dwell in the magnificent gardens prepared for it, to bask in His glory and remain in His presence for all eternity.

The new religion attracted some of the residents of Mecca, especially the younger ones, who would gather in the home of one of them, Al-Arqam, and listen to Muhammad's impassioned sermons, confirming their devotion to the almighty God and their absolute submission to Him and their readiness to carry out His will by bowing deeply and prostrating themselves until their foreheads touched the ground.

## A Ban

These gatherings did not attract the attention of the dignitaries and notables of the city-state, who hardly related to them at all. At least not until the number of Muhammad's adherents swelled and reached about seventy, and his sermons became directed explicitly against the wealthy and powerful, who he claimed were exploiting the miserable poor of Mecca, while indulging themselves in luxuries, debauchery, and other sins. The talented preacher did not stop at stating the facts, but went so far as to warn the sinners that if they did not repent and abandon their perverted ways while there was still time, their inevitable fate would be to burn forever in the fiery furnaces of Hell.

The notables of Mecca gathered in consultation, and being confident that they understood these people who were in no way different from themselves, offered Abu Al-Qasim Muhammad Ibn Abd Allah Ibn Al-Muttalib Ibn Hasim a considerable share of their trading profits and an additional wife from among the best and most noble young ladies of Mecca, as a suitable substitute for his new religion and as unequivocal appreciation of his blessed talents.

To their unpleasant surprise and deep and scorching distress, their proposal was rejected outright by the gifted preacher, and in a decisive, insulting and incontestable manner. The dignitaries of Mecca realized the extent of the danger that they were facing, and the fact that it was imminent. They convened again, and decided to eradicate the new religion and its preacher before it could flourish and extend its malignant shoots into the heart of every fool, rich or poor. So said these eminently wise men, and so they did, declaring a ban on the Hashemite clan – which this vigorous preacher stemmed from and belonged to – for not withdrawing their patronage from their errant and rebellious son, and instead of casting him out, had promised to continue to support him in all his erroneous ways.

The ban remained in force for three consecutive years, but like any such ban in the East, lost its momentum and passion with the passage of time, paled, faded and finally died a merciful death and was forgotten. It seemed that everything had ended peacefully and that the new religion would no longer be persecuted, nor would its preacher be estranged. Fate, however, has its own agenda and its own mysterious ways.

In the same year that the ban expired of itself, so too, one after the other, did Muhammad's wife, Khadigah, and his uncle, Abu Talib, his fierce and stubborn protector.

Abu Talib's place as head of the Hashemites was taken by Abu Lahab, who increasingly inclined toward the more moderate party and the more realistic Meccan faction, those that had banned the nascent prophet.

It turned out that without clan protection, the public that sought new ideas and cleaved to Muhammad's new religion disappeared as well.

Muhammad was constrained either to remain silent or to distance himself from Mecca, his birthplace.

The passionate preacher preferred distance to silence.


## The Hegira

The year 622 C.E., known as "The Year of the Hegira", is the first year of the Islamic calendar. On the 16th of July of that year, Muhammad departed Mecca, where rumor had it that he was about to be assassinated, and headed toward Medina, accompanied by a small troop of followers. It was a strange party that moved dejectedly over the familiar paths that traversed the desert, in silence, reflecting the desert's own silence.

As the sun rose on the twenty-fourth day of September in the first year of Islam, the party reached the outskirts of Medina, whose scattered houses were fortified against recurring attacks by marauders and migrating tribes seeking living space.

Strange as it may sound, it is a historical fact that until that year, and for some time after, the great majority of Medina's residents were Jews.

## A Trap

Three armed riders emerge from behind one of the houses, gallop toward the migrants, pull up their noble steeds at some distance with a masterful maneuver that attests to their superb horsemanship, and signal to the meager caravan to halt. It is immediately clear that these riders are free men, that they are at home here and that they have no intention of attacking or harming the visitors.

Muhammad and his followers halt.

One of the riders approaches at a light, noble trot, and greets them with the three blessings of the desert – the blessing of God, the blessing of the person speaking the blessing, and the blessing of those accompanying him.

The man facing Muhammad is slender and tall, with a smooth forehead, his deep-set eyes projecting intelligence, his calm and restrained gaze bespeaking self-control; the beard descending to his breast is combed and auburn, like the hair of his head, which is wrapped in a white turban, as is the custom of the Jews. He apologizes for the interruption which, he says, is ultimately to the benefit of the visitors, and explains: at a distance of some two hundred cubits a trap has been set for a gang of robbers that is expected to attack their settlement. It would thus be better for them to leave the familiar road and circle around the trap so as not to fall into it.

The man smiles, exposing two rows of alabaster teeth; a broad and fearless smile of welcome. His name: Zabir Ben Bata, a Jew by religion.

Muhammad, who is unknown in these parts, shows interest in Zabir the Jew, and even likes him, and it never occurs to him that fate, that same fate which the Qur'an will praise and condemn in the same breath, will yet bring them together again under the strangest of circumstances.

Muhammad asks: When are these robbers expected to attack?

The answer: At any moment.

May I watch?

If it is your wish.

One of the messenger-prophet's companions hastens to ask the Jew if there is any danger in watching.

The answer: Dangers lurk in all corners of life.

Muhammad dismisses the timorous question of his companion with a wave of his hand, and the latter goes back to his place. Muhammad then turns to Zabir and thanks him, and signals to his caravan to follow the three Jewish riders. Soon they behold a settlement surrounded by well-tilled fields, cultivated vineyards and well-watered vegetable gardens, where the rays of the sun gleam as they break on the dewdrops.

Zabir points out a broad strip of dark colored soil at the edge of the fields that reaches to where their horses had stood, and explains that under the soil spread over thin and fragile boards of wood and palm branches that look as if scattered at random, there is a deep trench.

Before Zabir manages to complete his explanation, a hundred or a hundred and twenty riders charge out from behind a hill to the west, screaming wildly and waving their swords, and gallop directly toward the fields and the houses, whose whitewashed walls calmly reflect the light of the newly risen sun.

Muhammad witnesses the decisive defeat of the sword-wielding troop as they fall in droves into the camouflaged trench, dragging each other and their horses into it. Within minutes, it seems, the entire gang is destroyed, and the few who have managed to halt their steeds with the help of their lances turn their backs and ride for dear life in the direction from which they came. The defenders leave their ambush and pursue them on horse or foot, and all who are caught pay with their lives for their foul deed.

Muhammad and his followers are fascinated.

They express their praise and admiration for the acuteness of the Jews, and bid farewell to the three riders. Muhammad grasps the hand and elbow of Zabir, a sign of the friendship he feels for him, and Zabir responds in kind. Then Muhammad addresses Zabir and reveals to him who he is, and invites him to visit him at his home whenever he so wishes.

## Thabath Ben Kis the Ishmaelite

Muhammad and Zabir Ben Bata part, and each goes his own way, to attend to his own business.

A week later, Zabir travels to Mecca with some neighbors, Jews and Ishmaelites. In the teeming markets of Mecca all kinds of stories are being told about Muhammad, maligning him and calling him by all the loathsome names imaginable, which the Arabic language so abounds in. In those days, anyone who mocked Muhammad was considered a hero.

A neighbor-acquaintance of Zabir, Thabath Ben Kis the Ishmaelite, is trying to controvert the maligners and to contend with the slander they are spreading about Muhammad, whose teachings he has accepted and whose words he sees as the words of the living God. When he discovers that every sentence that he utters gives rise to renewed waves of boastful, roaring and ear-splitting laughter, Thabath, agitated and offended to the very depths of his soul, lets fly a stream of insults at the deriders and informers, threatening them with the burning furnaces of Hell. And in so doing, he goes too far. Suddenly these ignorant and frightened idlers fall upon him, and within seconds Thabath is flat on his back, pinned to the ground by dozens of hairy and muscular arms, unable to move a limb. Someone draws a long dagger that glints in the dazzling sunlight and, holding its grip in both hands, raises it high, shrieking wildly, proclaiming that Thabath's fate is to be the same as that of Muhammad, his Prophet, and that the blood of both will be spilled on the filthy ground and their corpses will be food for pigs and dogs.

The dagger, raised with great force, is aimed toward Thabath's heart, while he lies helplessly on the ground. It descends like lightning – but misses its mark.

A bowstring hums and an arrow aimed by a master archer pierces the heart of the dagger-wielder, who collapses lifeless on top of Thabath. The market toughs, together with those who had sought the death of Muhammad's fervent follower, scatter and flee for their lives. Casual passers-by who are gifted with practical wisdom and the rich experience of life that the desert imparts in abundance flee in all directions, dragging their beasts after them. The stall-owners cover their goods, lock their stalls and miraculously vanish.

Only Thabath, the dagger-wielder's corpse with a reddening stain spreading beneath it, and the marvelous archer, still mounted, remain in the empty alley.

Thabath throws off the fresh corpse, turns to seek his savior, runs to him, prostrates himself at his horse's hoofs and kisses the earth beneath them. Jumbled words of gratitude, praise, promises and vows pour out like a fountain from his parched mouth. The savior, sitting on his horse like a statue, is none other than Zabir Ben Bata, the Jew.

## The Prophet and His Follower

Upon returning to Medina, Thabath rushes to prostrate himself at the feet of Muhammad, his Prophet, and tells him in detail about what happened to him in Mecca, about his own deeds and about the malice of its residents and their mood and their declared hatred of God's Prophet and of his God, their sins and transgressions which attest to their being the sons of Hell, whence they arose and whither they will return, and last, but not least, marvelous and astonishing – how by the hand of Allah, blessed be He, in His boundless and infinite mercy, an angel was sent from Heaven to save him, and the name of this marvelous angel is Zabir Ben Bata, the Jew.

Muhammad remains silent for a long time. Then he gestures to Thabath to rise from the floor, praises his faith and loyalty, and predicts wonders and marvels for him because of his powerful devotion to Allah, blessed be He, His laws and injunctions, and his constant battle against the greatest of sins, which is pride. As for Zabir Ben Bata the Jew, it is evident that an angel from Heaven had indeed descended to him at the last and decisive moment, drawn his bow, shot his arrow, and saved the life of a true Muslim... In complete reverence, humility and submission, Thabath asks his Prophet, the messenger of God, whether an angel from Heaven, who is pure and noble, and constantly in the presence of Allah, blessed be He, could descend, even for a brief moment, to dwell in an impure body with an erring and a sinful soul?

The unequivocal answer to the question posed by Thabath, the pure Muslim, is: No.

If so – continues Thabath in the same vein of reverence and humility – then there is something within this Zabir Ben Bata, something pure, in spite of his being a Jew!

Again the prophet is silent. Then he sighs, turns to his follower and asks him to convey to Zabir Ben Bata his blessing and his good wishes and gratitude for his righteous deed and the correct way he had dealt with his neighbor, and to invite him to him, to Muhammad, though not to partake of food, for the Jews still persist in their worthless custom, a product of arrogance and haughtiness, of not sitting at the same table with people of other religions, except for conversation only. And by the grace and mercy of Allah – Muhammad explains to Thabath – he may undergo a change of heart, and the light of this excellent man Zabir Ben Bata may shine, and perhaps his redemption will be hastened and God will grant him the wisdom to understand his place and his destiny.

## The Encounter

Zabir has accepted Muhammad's invitation and comes to visit him at his home in Medina, one of those fortified houses whose walls have never been breached by unwelcome strangers.

The two men are sitting in the inner courtyard of the house, under an ancient tamarisk whose spreading branches provide a thick shade, facing an eye-refreshing fountain. The conversation flows pleasantly.

Zabir is well-versed in the Jewish Torah, and Muhammad, who knows something about it, is trying to delve into its depths and understand some of its subtleties.

Is it possible to be a prophet of the Jewish Torah, and what does it involve?

The answer: With great suffering. No prophet was ever sent to a nation or group of people who keep God's commandments, but only to those who have abandoned God's path, which illuminates and straightens the crooked path of the evil impulse.

May the laws of the Torah be changed, to make it easier for the people suffering under their burden, and to show them a new way?

The answer: No.

"Torah from Sinai" means – all that is written therein has been written by the finger of God and not one jot may be changed nor any deviation countenanced.

And what about interpreting this Torah, in a manner that will attract the masses so that even other nations would join the Jewish faith and cleave to it – would such interpretation be considered heresy?

There exist all sorts of interpretations, too many to count. A broad range of opinions and concepts which at times contradict one another. Interpretations are of no decisive importance.

Nonetheless, says Muhammad, I am a messenger and a prophet, and God has called me to break a new path to the hearts of his creatures.

If so, then it is not to Jewish hearts.

The hearts of the Jews are hard! – Muhammad stresses.

Zabir Ben Bata falls silent, and Muhammad adds:

It was they who wholeheartedly wished the death of Jesus of Nazareth and even brought about his crucifixion!

Some of them – Zabir Ben Bata responds earnestly – the first Christians were all Jews. So were the Apostles, and Jesus of Nazareth himself, and his mother too.

And yet, today there is hatred between Jews and Christians!

The guest fixes his gaze on the mosaic in the yard, without responding.

Muhammad stands up and warns his guest explicitly: If the Jews do not listen attentively and try to understand the new true faith, and do not take part in its construction – they will taste the sword! Zabir rises, gazes calmly into Muhammad's blazing eyes, and states in a clear voice: No true religion was ever disseminated by the power of the sword.

The conversation has ends.


### "Razias"

Mecca is boiling with excitement. Its notables decide to teach a lesson to their errant and rebellious son who sees himself as the Prophet of God and His supreme messenger, and is inciting their slaves and servants against them. There can be only one sentence for the pretender Muhammad – to be lowered into a burial pit, and the sooner the better.

Rumors about all that is happening in Mecca reach Muhammad, who is surrounded by his followers and immersed in his prayers, at the spacious house that has been placed at his disposal for him and his children and wives. Nonetheless, he makes time to find a suitable response to the threats issuing from Mecca. He knows well that the Meccans claim, and the entire world believes, that they are protected in their commerce, their manufacture, and in everything they do, and that no one will harm them, due to the sanctity of the Ka'aba, that ancient structure in their city about whose holy origins so many legends have been spun.

If Muhammad were to succeed in harming the Meccan caravans, the legend will be shattered and its aura will descend to dust, and there will no longer exist a power in the world that as-it-were protects them and makes them holy and sanctified, invulnerable, always victorious and invincible.

Muhammad orders the conducting of "razias" – raids or sorties – on the caravans traveling to and from Mecca. In the year 632 C.E., Muhammad in person leads three of these "razias", which is a borrowed name and a euphemism for a totally stark reality, whose ancient, precise and well-known name is "robbery", or more correctly, "armed robbery".

## A Rift

Muhammad is determined to subdue Mecca by means of the "razias" or, at least, to use them as preparation for his approaching victory over it. Those engaged in commerce, from Yemen in the south to Syria in the north, are furious. The strongest opposition and most vocal protests come from the Jewish households. This opposition and open criticism put an end to Muhammad's lukewarm attitude toward the Jews. One of the fundamental rules of Islam, that of facing in the direction of Jerusalem during prayer, is revoked, and replaced by the holy injunction, which is extant to this day, to pray in the direction of the Ka'aba in Mecca.

The Jews of Medina and its surroundings are unwilling to abandon their birthplace, even though they sense the increasing hostility of Muhammad's followers and the approaching calamity. In order not to arouse anger, and in the hope that the disagreements will be somehow smoothed away, they do not unite into large camps or try to coordinate among themselves. Medina is holy to them because of the grave of Aaron, Moses' brother, which they visit and tend and prostrate themselves upon it on holidays and festivals. It is also told of the Jews of Medina that their forefathers had put down roots in the oasis as long ago as the time of King Solomon, and it appears that they mediated between the Queen of Sheba and the royal house in Jerusalem. Each household in Medina kept a splendid genealogical tree scroll, which they preserved in the family archives for centuries.

## A Zabir-Like Trap

At first, the "razias" were not very successful, and the Muslims paid for their daring dearly, with many casualties, and their self-confidence was shaken. Could this be the will of God? But they soon acquired skill in their ancient-renewed vocation, and slowly but surely began to gain the upper hand. The Meccans, as well as other merchants coming from and going to Mecca, were robbed according to all the unwritten rules of the art of armed robbery. The legend that all who traveled to and from Mecca are protected by the holy Ka'aba was shattered to smithereens.

There was no longer any avoiding an open and decisive confrontation between the Muslims ensconced in Medina and its surroundings and their opponents, the angry Meccans.

The Meccans organized a punitive expedition, a mighty army in terms of those days, ten thousand riders, skilled swordsmen all. The rumors of this took wing and reached Muhammad. The prophet recalled the Jewish warrior, Zabir Ben Bata, and the trap that he had set for the robbers, and copied his idea precisely, but with one important addition: Muhammad ordered the harvesting of the crops, so that there would be no feed for the starving horses on the way.

On the appointed date, the Meccans emerge in a screaming horde, galloping madly, and fall, some into the Zabir-like trap, and others – into Muhammad's trap. And as if this is not enough, a strong wind rises and torrential rain pours down on the attackers. There are those who say that Allah assisted His Prophet from the Heavens, while others comment that had it not been for the stormy weather, the Muslims would have pursued the Meccans, slaying them in vast multitudes. One way or another, the unavoidable and incontestable result is defeat of the Meccans.

Muhammad is victorious. And now, without delay or hesitation, the messenger-prophet turns his bloody sword and his army – which has swelled to thirty thousand swordsmen, against the Jews. If the Jews wish to save themselves, Muhammad leaves them a narrow and dirty opening, imprinted with the mark of disgrace – to crawl at his horse's hoofs, to reject their Judaism, and to convert to and accept Islam. And the intention is that even as converts and Muslims they will be discriminated against and differentiated from the rest of the "faithful", and will be pointed at as desecrators of a holy covenant, to the end of time, as this is practiced by Christianity and among the Christians. If the Jews' honor is dear to them, then there is only one sentence for them: death for the men, slavery and servitude for the women and children.

This ultimatum was presented to every Jewish community in the Arabian peninsula, except for the Karaite tribe, who were attacked without being offered any conditions, fought desperately and fell on the battlefield, while those who were captured were cruelly slaughtered.

## Arab Sources

The victorious Muslim army stands at the very outskirts of Medina, where in 622, the first year of the Hegira, the Prophet had encountered Zabir Ben Bata, the Jew.

The prophet-messenger, girded with sword, proclaims a reprieve for every Jew who converts to Islam. And this is how the event was described by Arab sources that certainly cannot be accused of any favoritism toward the Jews:

"Muhammad sent word to the Jews that if they accept the faith of Islam, no harm shall befall them. Three or four of them did as he said, and saved themselves, but all the rest heeded the words of their rabbi, Khiyai, not to betray their religion, the heritage of their forefathers, whatever might befall them. They prepared to give up their lives for the sanctity of their God, but did not venture to fight for their lives, thinking that perhaps Muhammad would be merciful, since they had surrendered to him, and would grant them their lives."

Indeed, their hope was not unfounded, for unlike other Jewish communities, they had never provoked Muhammad or taken a stand against the Muslims, their neighbors and friends, and were considerate of them and listened seriously to what they had to say. Nonetheless, the Prophet of Islam and leader of the Muslims, victorious in battle, told them clearly: whoever did not join him would receive no mercy.

The Arab eye-witness continues his description with a strange equanimity and a noteworthy objectivity hardly typical of the peoples of the East, and adds yet another foundation for their nurturing that ancient disastrous hope: "And it was when they opened their gates, the clan of Aus, who in the past had been allies of the Jews, approached Muhammad and asked him to grant the Jews a reprieve, as he had done to the Kinka'a clan at the request of the Hurj clan."

Indeed, there was an apparently solid

foundation for that hope, which is best not named or defined in words: there exists a precedent. Muhammad had shown mercy on the Jews who were allies of the Hurj, a well-known and respected Ishmaelite clan, and had reprieved them instead of putting them to the sword. Why, then, should he not act so here, by the same standard? The Aus clan, no less respected than the Hurj clan, and likewise true Muslims and allies, submit their petition, that very same petition that had been submitted by the Hurj clan, for a reprieve for their allies, the Jews, who have already proven their loyalty to Muhammad by disarming and announcing their unconditional readiness to accept his judgment, be it unfavorable, that is, to be slaughtered, or merciful. And as for conversion, it is a matter of honor. The precepts of forefathers and an ancient tradition are not something to be taken lightly, and one who shrugs them off under any threat shows himself to be not a person of stature who can be trusted. On the contrary, it is those people who have converted because of the circumstances, who have sold their birthright for a mess of pottage, from whom one can expect dark conspiracies, malice, weakness and betrayal.

Marvelous arguments, and – from the standpoint of pure justice and basic human dignity – solid and quite incontrovertible, and no upright, generous and noble person would rule against them. Except Muhammad.

Muhammad listens very attentively to the honorable clan of Aus, remains silent when they conclude their plea, like one who deliberates and weighs various arguments and possible solutions, and finally speaks and states his judgment in a manner which is far from harsh, showing not the slightest bit of favoritism, nor a hint of cruelty. Neither does it harm the Aus clan in any manner, nor the Jews who have surrendered to him, meaning that nothing in Muhammad's decision directly injures the Jews who have willingly laid down their arms, faithful to some mysterious impulse of those possessing neither motherland nor birthplace, hoping to arouse his compassion and be granted his mercy.

The eye-witness continues, adds and describes:

"Muhammad answered them: 'I will not be the judge of this matter, and will hand the decision over to Sa'ad Ibn Ma'ad, one of your people (of the Aus clan - S.K.) and whatever he deems right will be done!'"

No judgment could have been more neutral in its considerations or a clearer attempt at uncompromising adherence to justice and to justice alone; this is the objectivity of an incorruptible judge who goes to the heart of the matter and is cautious not to pronounce a hasty or improper sentence. All of the evidence, the arguments and the facts have been taken into account. Except, of course, for the fact that among all of the honorable Aus clan, Sa'ad Ibn Ma'ad is the only one who nurtures a deep hatred of the Jews, who had wounded him in battle, and his wounds, which were bloody, have not yet healed, and still hurt. And Muhammad knew this.

Sa'ad Ibn Ma'ad does not deliberate, does not wait for a second invitation, loses not a single second, and decrees on the spot:

"This is my sentence – the men are to be slaughtered and the women and children are to be sold in the slave markets."

And all the entreaties, arguments and promises of Sa'ad Ibn Ma'ad's own clan were of no avail.

The faithful eye-witness adds, and emphasizes:

"And Muhammad said (to Sa'ad Ibn Ma'ad – S.K.):

"'You have spoken well, and Allah has agreed with you as well, as He has revealed to me just now.'"

Allah has approved as well. There is no higher court of appeal, no longer anyone to turn to. The wheels of Muslim justice, as distinct from non-Muslim justice, grind quickly, leaving no room for speculation or reflection.

The eye-witness continues and discloses:

"The Jews sat in the Asama courtyard with their hands bound. Their women and children were locked in the Bint-Harath courtyard. The men stood all night praying to God... Every man helped to strengthen his brother not to betray their faith, but to die with courage in martyrdom sanctifying the Holy Name."

A most familiar sight, known, shameful, which is to be repeated many more times and to become a routine of sorts from then on until the Second World War. And if those who are willing to die for no crime that they have committed are called holy, then most of the children of this people are holy, "a holy nation", to cite the Old Testament prophet.

The reliable Arab source continues his description in his succinct, somewhat clumsy manner, or, more correctly, in a manner free of literary pretension or brilliance:

"Early in the morning of the following day, Muhammad gave orders to dig deep pits in the marketplace, and to bring out the Jews. There they slaughtered them and tossed their corpses into the pits. The horrible slaughter continued throughout the day." It appears that the Arab eye-witness too was horrified by the gruesome sight, and he deviates from the objectivity of his dissertation and his considered words and deems it proper to add the adjective "horrible" to the word "slaughter". "The horrible slaughter continued throughout the day," he writes, and adds accurately and untiringly, "and also at night they slaughtered Jews by torchlight, until they had slaughtered them all, some six hundred in number." How this chronicler performed the count remains his own secret. But here it is, the number, which he felt obliged to pass on in his authentic story to the world and to generations to come.

It appears that at this point the chronicler is overcome by pity, and he decides to relate an event that took place in the course of "this horrible slaughter":

"One woman, on seeing her husband slaughtered, called out loudly to the slaughterers: 'Know that when you surrounded our home, a stone was thrown, wounding one of the Muslims in the head – it was I who threw the stone, tell that to your prophet!'"

The woman's words are transmitted as spoken to the Muslim leader, before whose eyes the slaughter is being conducted.

After a brief moment, the decision is made:

"Muhammad sentenced the miserable woman

to death."

And the narrator, who also witnessed the woman's death, concludes: "And (the woman - S.K.) died courageously and calmly, for she did not wish to continue living after her husband's death."

## On the Road to Medina

Zabir Ben Bata is not among those slaughtered nor among those who have converted and escaped with their lives. During these calamitous days, Zabir is traveling in the north on business, together with a neighbor and relatives. God has blessed his endeavors and the revenues are satisfactory, and Zabir is returning on the horse trail that leads to Gaza and from there to Mecca and Medina. He delays in Gaza, to buy his wife some Indian cloth which is pleasing to both sight and touch, as well as a skillfully crafted Egyptian gold bracelet. For his children, Zabir buys sweetmeats, tanned leather for shoes, and head-ornaments of Gazan make for the older daughters.

This accomplished, the entire party heads for home.

Did something distress them? Were they tormented by some prophesy, some nightmare, a sense of catastrophe, a hyena following them stubbornly, an omen of disaster?

We will never know.

There are no sources that can testify about the mood of that party of Jews returning to Medina, their home for generations, and even Zabir himself, who could read and write, has left us not a word. Or, if he inscribed a sentence or two on some scroll, it remains undiscovered.

When they are deep in the Arabian desert, a day's ride from Medina, the group encounters a solitary Jew, worn out, his face tormented and his eyes staring in bewilderment. They bless one another in the customary way, and the Jew is invited to sit down with them to partake of food. They slice the bread, say the blessing, speak of this and that. The Jew remains silent. He avoids their eyes and it can be clearly seen that he is frightened. They try to arouse him to speak. Finally he responds, and pours forth all that he has been holding back, and everything becomes clear. The Muslims are slaughtering the Jews and will spare no one. And the Jews, who have not organized themselves properly to face the calamity, are being killed in battle and butchered like lambs led to the slaughter... He himself –God has been merciful to him and allowed him to escape... His home is indeed not far from Medina, to the west of it, while they – their homes are to the east of it... The slaughterers have reached there as well... He knows that the men are imprisoned in the Asama courtyard after laying down their arms at Muhammad's feet... and perhaps they have all been slaughtered by now. The women and children will be sold into slavery, as is the custom. There is no escaping this disaster!

The Jewish guest doesn't touch the bread. Agitated, he adjures his hosts, asking them to vow not to return to Medina, but to turn away and head north. Their brethren the Jews who live there will comfort them in their calamity! They must not dare to go down to Medina! – he stresses in a parched voice, and it is clear that he is concerned for them and that his entire tale is true.

The men in the group are stunned. They stare into each other's eyes as if seeking assistance from one another. Clearly, they must make a fateful decision. And no decision can bring relief.

They do not finish their meal, but say their blessings hastily and almost by rote, and silently mount their steeds.

Zabir's four companions turn about and join the refugee. He himself returns to the familiar horse trail, which descends southward towards Medina.

Broad and severe is the desert, and its silence is

not to be violated. The sunset sets the horizon ablaze, until it turns to ashes and is no more. The sky is dismal. Zabir's head is bent, his heart gripped in a black vise of impending doom.

What has befallen his wife Esther, his sons, his daughters, are they still living?... He doesn't reply to his own question. It is superfluous to ask. God is great. Yet his people have betrayed Him. They have sold Him in their greed for profit.

Silently and secretly the shadows spread, lengthen, thicken. It is already dark. His lungs seem to refuse to inhale the cooling air, as if it were not air for breathing but a thousand sharpened slaughterers' knives. Slaughterers' knives in the hands of enemies who are trying to eradicate him from the land of the living. The sky is lower. Neither moon nor stars. A chill descends over all. A fierce chill.

Life and death – how tangible and how ordinary they are! What is beyond them arouses horror, wonder, and a strange hope.

His people have always sought to hold on to life, and their fate has always been death. And at times, much too often – a disgraceful death.

There is neither point nor purpose in such thoughts. Better to spur on his horse and hurry home, if he still has a home.

As if reading his thoughts, the horse breaks

into a gallop and the wind whistles by its ears. This is much better, without introspection, without thoughts, without assumptions, without a plan of action.

The distance shrinks. At this rate, barring some disaster, he will reach Medina before dawn.

### Zabir Ben Bata

Our eye-witness goes on:

"And a local Jewish man, Zabir Ben Bata by name, had saved the life of the Muslim Thabath Ben Kis. And Zabir came to Thabath and said to him:

"'Do you still remember me, Thabath?'

"And Thabath replied:

"'How could I forget my benefactor who was so charitable to me?!'

"And Zabir said:

"'A good person will be charitable to his benefactor. You know that I am in great trouble – do whatever is in your power on my behalf.'

"Thabath went to beg Muhammad to grant him Zabir's life. For this man had been a great benefactor to him, and now he, Thabath, wished to recompense him for his kindness. Muhammad did as he asked."

Did the former fugitive, migrant and outcast envision in his mind's eye the face of that Jew who had come out to warn him and prevent him from falling into the trap that had been set for another? Did the messenger-prophet, as he poured the foundations of a new religion, recall that illuminating conversation he had held in his home with that same Zabir, and the strong, indelible impression made on him by his interlocutor in his sincere grief at the fate of his own people?

The anonymous eye-witness, whose name may very well be Thabath Ben Kis – an assumption that in any case should not be dismissed outright – adds, and interprets:

"And Thabath returned in joy to tell Zabir of this (the pardon that he had secured for him from Muhammad - S.K.), but Zabir replied:

"'I have grown old, and have just lost my property, my wife and children are in bondage, what need have I of life?'

"And Thabath went to Muhammad and asked him about this as well.

"And the prophet acceded to Thabath's entreaties, and Thabath returned to Zabir with great joy and told him:

"'Your property will be restored to you and your wife and children will be given their freedom!'

"And Zabir asked Thabath:

"'Tell me, what was the fate of Assad Ben Ka'ab, whose face was always radiant and illumined like a polished mirror, who when seen by virgins blushed red from shame?'

"'Put to death!' replied Thabath.

"'And what of Hai Ben Ahtab, a hero in war and a mainstay in peace, who commanded an army in wartime and sang songs of peace when all was tranquil?'

"'Put to death!' replied Thabath.

"'And what of the hero Aza'el Ben Samil, who always charged at the head of the army in war, and when the people returned from battle was the rearguard behind the entire camp?'

"'Put to death!' replied Thabath.

"'And what of Nabash Ben Kis, crafty as a fox and a man of many subterfuges, who always found the hiding place of anyone who escaped him, and there was no knot which he could not untie?'

"'Put to death!' replied Thabath.

"'And what of Akaba Ben Zayid, the hospitable, father to the orphans and the poor?'

"'Put to death!' replied Thabath.

"'And are the two wise men, both named Amar, who always sat and studied the Torah, still alive?'

"'They too were put to death!' replied Thabath.

"'If so – said Zabir – what need have I of life? It would be better for me to be gathered to the bosom of my people with those who have preceded me in their deaths. One thing I will ask of you, Thabath my friend, take me to the marketplace, and behead me there with my sword, for it has been sharpened. I am old and weary, and no longer wish to live. Grant me this favor!'

"'I cannot!' Thabath replied.

"'If you are unable to do this for me, then hand me over to be slain by one of your men; but go to your leader and ask him for kindness to my wife and children. And see to it that he restores to them the property which I have acquired.'

"And Thabath did as his friend asked: he handed over Zabir to Awan, who slew him, but Zabir's wife and children he took into his own home."

# SAINT JANUSZ' GARDEN

## The Outlaws

The Turkish word *Kozak* (Cossack) has no parallel in Western or Eastern languages. Its meaning, in part, is "adventurer," just as it might be "freedom lover" or "outlaw." The Turks used it to refer to groups of rebellious peoples who, in the fifteenth century, left crowded and institutionalized population centers, and turned to the wide open steppes of the Don and Dnieper regions, and further on, splitting up as they advanced, until they reached the Caspian Sea in the north and the Caucasus Mountains in the south. Although they would not suffer any kind of institutionalized framework, if anyone invaded their territories they were quick to muster into fighting units, to meet the invaders, attack them and, in most cases, drive them out of their fertile lands. In times of peace they worked the land, raising cattle and, especially, horses. In horse riding they were second to none.

The question of their ethnic origins is not sufficiently clear, and is a matter of controversy. There are those who claim that they descend from the Tartars, while others swear by everything holy and prove by signs and omens that pure Slavic blood runs in their veins. The truth, probably, is somewhere in between: they are a unique mixture of the Slav and the Tartar, with a variety of results, at times noble, at other times disgusting.

That which unites all the Cossacks, wherever they may be, is their religion. The Cossacks, it turns out, of their own free will and the inclinations of their hearts, took the Christian religion upon themselves. And of all the Christian churches, they chose the Greek Orthodox Church. The Cossacks excel in their piety, which has never been a matter of mere rote. In the churches, at the feet of icons, in the field or at home, in times of peace as in wartime, the hardened Cossack kneels and prays, bareheaded, crying and sobbing in the intensity of his remorse and his feelings of guilt, asking for forgiveness, making solemn vows, and repenting. A short time afterwards, before his tears have dried, that same man gallops off to a nearby town to take booty and to plunder, to rape, to destroy and put to fire everything that crosses his path, and to slaughter people, especially if they are Jews.

## The Gentry

To Poles, nothing is more precious than honor. This is the gleaming honor, displayed for all to see. *"Niemam pieniadze, mam honor",* "I have no money, but I have honor," – an ancient and quite common Polish proverb.

Thomas Mann, in his book *The Magic Mountain,* elucidates one aspect of this pride:

"It was a Polish matter, a fight over pride which took place in the bosom of the Polish community.... The group was so chivalrously elegant and polished that no one on the outside could but raise his eyebrows, and not be surprised by anything that might happen here," and, "Mr. Japol expressed things... which related to Mr. Von Zutawski's wife, as well as to a young lady named Krilov, who was related to Mr. Ludigowski," and, consequently, those who had been insulted came to the man who had insulted them, and slapped him several times in front of witnesses, all of which was recorded in the protocol and signed by those witnesses, and the protocol was then distributed, in the original (Polish) and in translation. Among other things, the quite long and exceedingly detailed protocol states: "... therefore, on April 2, 19..., between 7:30 and 7:45 p.m., in the presence of his wife, Jadwiga, and Messrs. Michael Ludigowski and Ignatz Von Melin, he (the offended person– S.K.) went up to Mr. Kazimir Japol, who was seated in the company of Mr. Janusz Theophil Linart and two unknown young ladies in the American bar of the local club, drinking alcoholic beverages, and slapped him in the face a number of times."

To collect witnesses in order to slap someone who least expected it, someone who was helpless and timid, and known as a coward, who would in any case not react – and to record this in a protocol.

### "Poland"

The root of the name "Poland," or "Polska" is the Slavic-Polish word *pole*, or, in the softer Russian pronunciation, *polye* – a field. A considerable part of Poland is fields and meadows. The Pole is a man of the fields, a farmer. This simplistic interpretation is not acceptable to many Polish scholars, and some have tried to prove that "field" is a synonym for "expanse," which is a synonym for freedom. Hence, Poland is the land of freedom, and the Pole is a man of freedom, a freeman by birth.

When the name of the Polish people comes up in the chronicles of mankind, note is made of its tendency to crowd together in centers where art, commerce, science, order and enlightened political thought can flourish, in complete contrast to their neighbors, the "outlaw" Cossacks, who escaped to the wild expanses and isolated themselves from the public.

The hatred and loathing between these two nations not infrequently led them to slaughter each other with a heated cruelty, and to persecute each other mercilessly. This might have yielded quite tragic results, were it not for a third factor which appeared on the scene. This third factor which, according to an ancient Roman proverb, should have benefited from the bitter enmity prevailing between these reluctant neighbors, became – by virtue of their ancient gift of arousing hate wherever their feet trod – a unifying factor.

## The Third Factor

"YiSRa'EL" ("Israel") – "(he who) wrestled with God", who attained to come so close to God as to touch Him. "YaShaR" – righteous, fair; "EL" – God, whence – "the righteousness of God is in him." "Yehuda" ("Judah") – thanksgiving, praise, dearness, devotion, joy in God, for God.

All these names, historical interpretations and philological analyses will not help, even in the slightest, to fathom the depths of the tortured and complex soul of "Israel", of the one and unique Jewish nation, which lived and existed before the world knew Rome and Greece, and continues to exist after their disappearance, in the same pattern, with the same fate. All human failings are found in this people; all human virtues have stemmed from it. The first Christians were Jews. All the Messiah's holy Apostles, his Blessed Mother, He Himself, were true sons of Israel.

The warrior-prophet of Islam drew his inspiration and his bravery of spirit from Jews and from Jewish scriptures. All the nations ostracize the people of Israel, and Israel, so it transpires to its misfortune, feels superior to all the nations, and scorns them.

There is no corner of the world where there are no Jews, and with the exception of a very few and quite strange ethnic groups, such as the Serbs, whose unique honor distinguishes them from all the nations – there is no people or nation or tribe among whom the Jews have not become hated. So strong has been the hatred that it penetrated the hearts of the hated and filled them with venom, until they came to hate themselves.

### A Shamed and Mournful Stream

The Jews appeared in regions inhabited by Slavic households before the latter became peoples and nations. A shamed and mournful stream of people, fleeing from the sword, from the Low Countries and Germany, France and Rome, Spain and Portugal. At first, they aroused curiosity, which turned into wonderment, and, in the natural course of things, after longer contact with these bearded men, with their tormented gaze and their sharp tongues, and their frightened, quite good-looking daughters, came the turn of hostility, animosity and hatred.

Both the Christian camps saw the Jews as exploiters. In reality, both exploited the Jews. The Cossacks simply robbed them, again and again. The Poles imposed exceptional taxes on them, and exploited them as their agents and tax collectors, which inflamed the hatred against them even more.

It is said of the Jews that they survive under all conditions, and that they would actually do anything to survive. But this is not true. Jews have been slaughtered, and are still being slaughtered in a manner that no other people has known or experienced, and they survive – in explicit contradiction to their will. In all the glorious and not so glorious annals of mankind, no other persecuted, humiliated and oppressed people has so frequently committed collective acts of suicide, or so often offered its neck to the executioner.

In their stiff-neckedness, which has become famed and is even mentioned with condemnation in the Scriptures, and in their zeal for outworn principles, the Jews astound the peoples of the world, and, above all – themselves. They are always on the losing side, yet to this day no people, language or nation that has waged war against them has not been vanquished by them. A people far from arousing sympathy, who brought to the family of nations the tidings about the existence of God and of His being Love, and banished the bearers of the tidings, sons of their own people, bone of their bone and flesh of their flesh. A people rejected and hated by everyone. God's people.

## The Situation

The seventeenth century was one of those centuries which held a blessing for the Polish people. Kings come and go, a duke is deposed, and another ascends, and the Polish cavalry goes on to expand the homeland's territories, till no one can authoritatively say where its borders are, and how great it is.

A Pole of the seventeenth century is a *pan* in the full sense of the word: he resides in a castle built by anonymous Cossacks, surrounded by Cossack body-guards, and casts dread over a large region of Russian, Ukrainian, Cossack and Jewish households. Unlike the Swedes, he is not assimilated among his subjects, but, on the contrary, he builds a steel partition of contempt and arrogance between himself and them.

### A "Registered" Cossack

The Poles despised and oppressed the Cossacks in every way and at every opportunity, while at the same time displaying what might be described as Christian mercy towards them, and when they found a Cossack who was distinguished from his brethren in one way or another, able to read and write, or possessing a gift for organizing things – they would advance and elevate him, bring him closer and "register" him, in other words, recognize his existence as an individual.

Only a "registered" Cossack was given rights by the Poles, and only on the explicit condition that he know how to serve them faithfully, acknowledge the mercy and kindness his masters showed him, and be grateful.

The registered Cossack was given the full right to stamp, trample upon, and oppress his brother

Cossacks, as well as to be stamped, trampled upon and oppressed by his masters, the providers of his bread.

## Khmelnytsky

Once there was a registered Cossack called Bogdan Khmelnytsky, who served his Polish masters with mixed feelings. They found in him some sparks of leadership and organizational capability, and appointed him a Guard Commander and leader of gendarmes against Cossack tax evaders, and against violators of the law, who were also Cossacks. One day a gleaming Polish officer reproached the crude-mannered though "registered" Cossack, and threatened him with his riding crop, to teach him a lesson.

The Cossack Bogdan Khmelnytsky evaded the raised whip, cursed the officer, left the barracks and – vanished. The Cossack gendarmes who hastily mounted their horses to pursue, capture and bring him to a Polish court for punishment, came back empty-handed. He was neither at home nor with his relatives. His friends knew nothing about him, his tribe almost denied him. One of his subordinates, after pursuing him in vain, remarked to the Polish officer that the wanted man had probably "gone down." To the officer's cutting question as to the meaning of "gone down", the Cossacks were perplexed. They scratched their heads, and tried to explain to His Excellency that "gone down" meant that he had gone underground, and could not be found until he decided, of his own free will, to come out of his hiding place and expose himself when he was ready and in the manner he deemed fit.

The Polish officer blew his nose loudly like a Cossack, ordered a guard to be put on Khmelnytsky's house and that of his parents, and, as soon as there was a suspicion that he was there, to break in and arrest the deserter, who could not escape Polish justice – the well-soaped knotted rope. Thus "His Excellency" dismissed the matter of Bogdan Khmelnytsky, disassociating himself from the miserable though "registered" Cossack who had "gone down" to the underground.

## The Revolt

As the Cossacks had said, Khmelnytsky came out of the underground of his own free will, when he was ready, and in the manner he deemed fit: as the leader of some tens of thousands of "unregistered" Cossacks, all excellent horsemen and famous swordsmen. As the first chapter of a highly suspenseful, vigorous and inspired play, he surprised the Poles at the fortified city of Kudak, took it by storm, and razed it to the ground. In May, 1648, aided by the Tartars, he defeated the Poles in open battle in the fields of Zhovti Vodi, and at Korsun. So began the famous revolt of Bogdan Khmelnytsky, one of a number of revolts by the Cossacks whom the Turks, in a rare moment of inspiration and perceptiveness, had defined as "outlaws" and "freedom lovers."

The revolt itself, with all its stages and upheavals, motives and ramifications, does not interest us here.

Our only intention is to put down in writing one of the events, based on solid facts, in which the three factors described at the beginning of our story took part or became involved in, willingly or unwillingly, and in the strangest manner.

### Rabbi Natan Neta Ben Moshe Hannover

The seventeenth century chronicler, Rabbi Natan Neta Ben Moshe Hannover, describes the Cossack revolt led by Khmelnytsky in 1648-9 not as an uninvolved observer or a disinterested objective witness, but as a Jew who has escaped by the skin of his teeth from the sword raised over his head by both the Cossacks and Poles, and then passes through the Polish Ukraine, hearing, seeing, and never ceasing to record. Finally the distinguished rabbi reaches Moravia, finds refuge in the city of Ungarish-Brod, far from the Poles and Cossacks, and gives a fervent sermon in the local synagogue. But he does not complete it: the sword of one of the Hungarian Kuruz, who in their attitude towards the Jews in no way fall short of the Poles and Cossacks, and could probably teach them a thing or two, lops off his head, and silences his lips.

One of the chapters in Rabbi Hannover's book *The Pit of Mire* – which, according to The Hebrew Encyclopedia, won him timeless fame – is dedicated to the fortress city of Tulczyn, which was not spared by Khmelnytsky's revolt.

## Tulczyn

Like every Polish fortress city in those days, the city of Tulczyn, located on the eastern border of the Ukraine, serves as a refuge for the Polish masters, whom Hannover refers to as "ministers." These, according to the recorder of the city's annals, number about six hundred "heroes", that is, about six hundred Polish households, and beside them, according to the same source, there are about two thousand Jewish households. Rabbi Hannover does not record the number of Cossacks in that city, from which it may be inferred that these were the attendants of the Polish "ministers," their servants, and slaves, and that they performed the same functions for the Jews as well. The Jewish community is headed by Rabbi Aaron, whose wisdom is also esteemed by the non-Jews, who come to him to settle their disputes and to receive judgment and, so it appears, are satisfied with his decisions. The Jews, unlike their brethren in always agitated Europe, deal in trade, but only of livestock, and mainly of horses. They have great knowledge of horses, and it must be said, to their exceptional credit, that they do not always cheat their customers. Some of them, too, are excellent riders of their well-groomed steeds, and even compete with Poles and with Cossacks, of whom it is said that they were born to the saddle, occasionally even unintentionally defeating them.

According to Rabbi Hannover, the Jews of Tulczyn did not fall short of the Polish "heroes," and knew how to use all the varieties of weapons known at the time, unlike their brethren in civilized Europe. Tulczyn had a *yeshiva,* headed by the same Rabbi Aaron, "The *Gaon* [Genius], Our Teacher and Master," who, according to Hannover, had sons and daughters, and at his side were the rabbis "The *Gaon*, Our Teacher and Master, Rabbi Eliezer," "The *Gaon*, Our Teacher and Master, Rabbi Shlomo," and "The *Gaon*, Our Teacher and Master, Rabbi Chaim," all of who had extensive families. And the House of Israel was happy and good of heart as much as it was possible to be happy and good of heart in the Exile and under the watchful eye of the Polish Duke Swierszczynski, governor of the city and commander of the garrison and the fortress, who needed the Jews and their services, and therefore controlled his natural loathing and suffered them.

The Jewish community at Tulczyn is prosperous, and the Polish Duke guarantees their safety and property, as long as they bring him and the Royal Treasury the profits expected of them.

Then the pastoral tranquility is disturbed, and the air becomes electrified, and the news that tens of thousands of Cossacks are headed for Tulczyn brings fear and trembling to the usually calm and sated inhabitants. The Polish "ministers" try in vain to put on an air of composure and self-confidence: the news of what is impending arouses anxiety in their hearts, and they are swept along with the masses of uneasy Jews who run through the alleys, crossing the market square back and forth, demanding that the "ministers" start ringing the bell as a signal of alarm. The ministers do as they ask, warn the population, and the gate-keepers hastily close their gates. Armed Poles mount the wall, and then it becomes clear to them how few they are, about six hundred sword bearers, according to Hannover, and they realize that it will not be easy to stand up to tens of thousands of Cossacks and drive them off.

### Rabbi Aaron

At this time of confusion and distress, The Gaon, Our Teacher and Master, Rabbi Aaron, goes to Duke Swierszczynski with a proposal which in other times and under different circumstances would have sounded strange, offensive and would have been rejected outright: the Tulczyn community's Chief Rabbi offers the help of the Jews to repel the Cossack attack, with one explicit condition – that both sides, the Poles and the Jews, vow, each before their God and according to their faith and customs, to be faithful to one another, not to betray each other, nor to discriminate between one kind of blood and another.

His Excellency Duke Swierszczynski

immediately grasps that in the present circumstances the Jewish rabbi's offer is no less than a gift from heaven. He is not happy about the matter of the vow, and tries to show the rabbi that he is insulted and very angry, but the rabbi does not relent. The Jews will not mount the walls and fight for the Polish city of Tulczyn without those ceremonies which as-it-were ensure their rear. The rabbi politely, but firmly, also refuses the "word of honor of a Polish nobleman" in place of a ceremonial vow. Even the implied danger of offending the honor of the Duke and the Polish people and their glorious King does not make the required impression on the rabbi. He repeats his demand that the ceremonies be conducted in full. This is the condition from which he will not swerve. The Duke therefore restrains himself with regard to the apparent insult, and invites the priests, and the rabbi invites the rabbis. The ceremony takes place, with all its details, according to law and custom.

**The Vow**

An ancient Torah scroll is brought from Tulczyn's main synagogue, and four rabbis swear upon it, in the name of all the Children of Israel, who are warranty for one another, to keep the faith with their Polish allies, and not to betray them. They call down upon themselves every curse should they transgress this sacred vow, and conclude by laying on hands and with awesome blowings of the *shofar.*

The Poles, too, vow in the name of the Father and the Son and the Holy Ghost to be faithful to their Jewish allies in the war with their common enemy, and not to betray them, and they too call down upon themselves every curse should they transgress this agreement in any manner.

Just as the ceremonies are ending, the lookout bursts into Duke Swierszczynski's luxurious reception hall, and announces that the Cossack army can be seen on the horizon, and is like locusts in number.

"To arms!" calls the Polish Duke fervently, drawing his sword and running to his troops.

The rabbis follow after him at a rapid pace. It turns out that almost every Jew has weapons hidden in the corner of a cellar or a pantry, and they hurriedly gird their swords, daggers and pistols, shoulder their muskets or bows and arrows, or take up their spears and pikes. They don armor which has become rusty, take up shields of all kinds, of various weights, materials and colors, and hasten to the wall. The Cossacks are already there, below them.

## The Battle

It is necessary to smash one more myth that people spread about the Jews out of mixed feelings of contempt, arrogance, curiosity, repulsion, malice and disregard of the facts: Jews do not loathe weapons, should they be lucky enough to find some in times of distress. Persecution follows persecution, catastrophe pursues catastrophe, holocaust leads to holocaust. Jews give up their lives, bare their neck to the axe, but also fight with weapons in their hands. Which of the three manners of extinction is heroic – everyone may judge for himself, and decide according to his own reasons. The Jewish people knows all three, being experienced in them like no other people.

At the head of the Cossack regiments charging furiously upon Tulczyn is a man of great resourcefulness and many stratagems, named Krywonos. The quite picturesque name is most accurate: this gifted commander, Jew-hater and zestful murderer of Poles has a crooked nose, as his name implies. On either side of this nose a pair of small gleaming eyes, black as pitch, the crafty eyes of a mouse, scurry about. His wide face and short and solid neck turn red from the great pleasure he gets from galloping on a horse into the roar of battle.

The Cossacks place tens of ladders against the fortress's walls, and climb them like demons. They are pushed back, with their ladders, and fall from a great height onto their backs. Only a few get up again. The Children of Israel and the "ministers" fight like lions. A few tens of Cossacks have succeeded in getting over the wall and are making their way towards the inner steps leading to the gates, vigorously brandishing their swords, emitting paralyzing cries and killing some of the defenders. But they are finally surrounded on all sides, completely cut off from their comrades, attacked with great fury, and pay for their bravery with their lives.

The Ataman Krywonos' first attack ends in failure. The Poles and Jews leaning against the wall and sitting beneath the embrasures look at each other in satisfaction. The Poles are surprised by the Jews' valor in battle. The Jews smile at their comrades-in-arms, a broad, hearty smile, which says: "Well, you have seen us now. This is what we are like! And if it depends on us, the Cossacks will not breach the wall, nor will a foot of theirs tread inside Tulczyn!"

The Jews of Magenza (Minz), too, in their time donned armor and girded weapons and fought the Crusaders who came to kill them, but, according to their chronicler, "Due to the many woes which befell them, and their fasting, they had no strength;" nor were they experienced in war, most of them being scholars and petty tradesmen, unfamiliar with the open air of the broad expanses, unlike the Jews of Tulczyn, and were all destroyed by the sword.

Krywonos returns and storms the wall with a new and yet more vigorous attack, planned in detail, and with increased forces. A few Tartars succeed in penetrating the wall, kill some of Tulczyn's defenders, and paralyze them for a brief while with their wild cries, which are accompanied by terrifying looks and swords raised with an executioner's skill. Tulczyn's defenders quickly recover, succeed in cutting the invaders off from their rear, and kill them without mercy, as they had done with their predecessors, and not a single one escapes alive.

## An Interval

It is a sunny day, the sun has already reached its zenith and is declining westward. Krywonos decides to offer an interval to the warriors of Tulczyn, who have proven their courage, and to himself and his own warriors, in order to freshen up, regain their strength and, mainly, to fill their bellies with whatever they require.


## Comradeship

The shared distress of Tulczyn's defenders creates situations that no one has imagined possible: Poles and Jews fighting shoulder to shoulder, completely forgetting that they are masters, "ministers," *"panie-s"*, and their despised agents. It turns out that the blood spilled in defense of their lives and the lives of the members of their households is exactly the same blood. Barriers cannot stand up to this test: they collapse and fall, as if they were never built, or never existed at all.

Abraham the Blacksmith, famous in Tulczyn and beyond as a superb craftsman, has revealed himself to be an excellent marksman and a swordsman none can compete with. Tall and firm of body, his stance is solid as a rock. His gaze is that of a shy virgin. Abraham turns to Wiaczeslaw, the handsome Polish officer with golden locks who is standing on the other side of the embrasure, and carries on a friendly conversation with him. Earlier, the attackers concentrated on the position manned by the two, tried desperately to ascend to it and kill its defenders, without success. Any Cossack or Tartar who stepped onto the broad upper surface of the wall fell dead before he had a chance to let out a cry, either by a shot from Wiaczeslaw's pistol, or by the swing of Abraham's great sword.

The dialogue is pleasant, and Abraham, who reads and studies the Torah and the Prophets, and is specially fond of the Ethics of the fathers, spices it with some heartening Jewish wisdom.

"Hey," says Abraham, turning to Wiaczeslaw, and a pink smile emerges and shows through his thick mustache and even-thicker beard, like a baby's smile, "let's have a competition."

"What about?" asks Wiaczeslaw, curious, returning a bright smile. Abraham wastes no time and clarifies in a clear voice, which can be heard for some distance:

"Which of the two of us will be the first to straighten Krywonos' nose, or to shave him clean, no matter in what way or with what weapon!"

"A brilliant competition!" Jews in nearby positions call out, and burst into loud laughter. The Poles follow close behind, and already a young fellow, a Yeshiva student, his long coat stained with blood, is standing there offering to take bets, "for Abraham or for Wiaczeslaw." It turns out that most of the Poles bet on Abraham. Then the young Rabbi Shlomo, who is considered a prodigy not only in the Torah but also in shooting and sword handling, gets up and bets on Wiaczeslaw. Rabbi Shlomo's followers hasten to bet as their rabbi has, and the forces are balanced.

Wiaczeslaw's young wife comes up to the wall, bringing her husband his hot meal in steaming casseroles. Without any formalities, the Polish officer invites Abraham to have a taste. To the surprise of all the Jews on the wall, and the amazement of the Poles, Abraham is not embarrassed, does not blush in shame or recoil, does not ask a rabbi's support or advice, does not emit a stammered excuse, even one lacking gross insult, to refuse the offer. Abraham the Blacksmith accepts the invitation, and, in knightly manner, eats of the meat, without even asking, at least, if it is pork.

Poles and Jews alike perceive that here, at this very moment, before their very eyes, an exceptional step has been taken, a change heralding hope has occurred, and, without accounting to themselves about their actions, burst out in a single voice with the shout: "For Abraham and Wiaczeslaw!," "For Wiaczeslaw and

Abraham!" Rabbi Shlomo sees fit to quote a passage of encouragement and praise for the blacksmith's deed, and speaks it aloud for all to hear, with the addition of an illuminating commentary. The wall resounds with loud cries of joy, hand-clapping, pats on the back and rolling laughter, attesting to what among all peoples and in all languages is called "comradeship."

## Love at First Sight

Governor Swierszczynski's daughter brings her father, who is standing on the wall, the holy book he had requested, though his hidden desire was to take pride in her and her beauty. The maiden's name is Ludmilla, and she is the only creature of female gender in Tulczyn and in all of the Polish Ukraine who has learned to read and knows how to write.

Ludmilla is eighteen years old, slender of figure, with light auburn hair that flows down to her shoulders in broad waves, a shining face that is milky in hue, and a forehead that is clear like a morning in spring. Her eyebrows are dark and straight, and beneath them are revealed two deep, pure springs of infinite mercy, courage and understanding. Like a ray of light that has deviated from a young star and come to the world to bring illumination to men, to encourage them and to ease their suffering – such is the maiden Ludmilla of the House of Swierszczynski.

Those who saw her rejoiced and were encouraged, and the Polish Governor was well satisfied. Now, something which the Governor did not expect or understand happened: the maiden Ludmilla's glance crossed that of Michael, the young son of Rabbi Aaron the *Gaon*, leader of the Jewish community of Tulczyn. Suddenly her white cheeks were inundated by a fierce blush, her step lost its harmonious lightness, and she stopped still as if rooted to the spot, not taking her eyes away from Michael's eyes, and it was clear that this was none other than love at first sight, pure and strong, and everyone saw this and were happy and joyful, except for the maiden's father.

The Duke approaches his daughter and takes the book, which is elegantly bound in an ivory binding. His face darkens, and he orders her to return to her mother immediately. The maiden Ludmilla obeys, hastening to carry out her father's command.

In the Governor's angry heart many thoughts arise, all revolving around the one subject: how to distance his daughter from Michael, or how to make it happen that Michael will never see his daughter again, or, for that matter, the city of Tulczyn, or the Ukraine, or Poland....

The Governor's wife, the Duchess Jadwiga, hears from her beloved daughter her agitated story about the Jewish boy with the sharp features, his high forehead, his black locks, his strong eyebrows, his dark eyes in which no wisdom in the world, nor any secret, are not reflected, the son of Rabbi Aaron, the wisest of all of the inhabitants of Tulczyn.

Duchess Swierszczynski is embarrassed. She cannot oppose her daughter's flood of emotions, and is swept along with her against her will. The Duchess understands that the matter is dangerous, extremely dangerous to both sides, and that from this unripe love, enchanting and strong enough to destroy worlds as it is, nothing worth benediction will grow.

**His Word is His Deed**

After they have sufficiently filled their bellies and snatched a brief sleep on the hard ground, the priest accompanying the Cossacks calls them to public prayer. Some of the Cossacks respond, kneel, bare their heads, and pray for a rapid victory over the Messiah's enemies, and for as much booty as possible; others vacillate, while some, not necessarily the minority, continue lying on their backs, pronouncing juicy oaths and known curses against the priest and his God, for daring to disturb their rest.

Krywonos is not impressed by either the prayers or the curses. He is weighing various considerations in his mind, and comes to the decisive conclusion that the city will not be taken by force nor by arms, and that all the frontal attacks in the world, as daring as they might be, will not help; the time has come to act differently, that is, to let guile make its voice heard, and for cunning to prove its value. Indeed, his bag contains a choice kind of guile, perhaps the choicest of all, the guile of a boor and a simpleton, which has a magical power that even the world's wisest men cannot withstand.

Krywonos is not one who vacillates, torments himself or convenes councils in order to reach the most sophisticated decisions by a majority of votes. He knows that "sit and do nothing" is incomparably more dangerous than "do," even if the "do" is in error from the outset and mistaken all the way. The Ataman with the ox-like neck and mouse-like eyes that gleam in their sockets says what is to be done, and his word is his deed.

Krywonos calls Simion, his second-in-command, who weighs as much as a fattened ox and not every horse is capable of bearing him, and Dimitri, the drunkard priest whose eyes are glassy green like a viper's and his body thin as a stick, and whose intellect, it turns out, is sharp, if of course he has imbibed enough alcohol. Krywonos briefly reveals to them that they are to go to the Poles and conduct negotiations with them. He does not ask them their opinion, nor does he try and check in any manner if they have understood what was said.

The three leave the Cossack camp. Krywonos rides in the middle, Simion to his left with a white flag in his right hand, and Dimitri to his right, with holy books in his black pouch.

## The Deputation

In the fortress they see the threesome with its white flag raised high, a sign of honest intentions, apparently a request to conduct negotiations, and the excitement is great. Could it be that they are requesting a truce? Perhaps they are sick of war, and have not finished burying their dead, and want nothing else but to be allowed to collect their dead, to bury them with dignity, to leave Tulczyn and go back to where they came from?

Or, perhaps, their intention is none other than to fool Tulczyn's defenders? This thought is what disturbs the tranquility of not a few warriors, not permitting happiness and hope to find a place in their hearts. And all those who are unquiet, suspicious and worried, are from among the Jews.

Wiaczeslaw, the handsome young officer, tries to calm his comrades-at-arms:

"There's no danger," he states with emphatic confidence. "The Cossacks are exceedingly stupid, and if they try something cunning, their plot will quickly become evident! Duke Swierszczynski has much experience with Cossacks, and knows them better than they know themselves! One such as he will not fall into a Cossack trap! There is also the Jewish Rabbi, Aaron the Genius, who is unequalled in all of Tulczyn and the Polish Ukraine in wisdom, understanding and knowledge!"

The young Pole's words are consoling, and the Jews on the wall return a hesitant, it might be said embarrassed, smile, to his own radiant and encouraging smile.

The strange trio comes within talking distance of the wall, stops, and Krywonos places his hands around his mouth, stands up straight in the saddle, and calls out in a thundering, guttural voice:

"We ask negotiation!" He repeats his call three times. After each call, his deputy waves the white flag, a piece of dirty sheet wrapped around a long crooked stick. The priest Dimitri raises his left hand, in which he holds one of the holy books he has removed from his greasy pouch made of blackening leather, and points to it with his right hand as if this book were a warranty of honest intentions and a sincere Christian request for peace.

A runner sets out urgently to summon the Governor, who leaps onto his horse, rides to the wall, climbs up onto it, grimly and with evident suspicion surveys the members of the deputation standing somewhere below, and commands his adjutant to answer:

"We are ready!"

"We're advancing to the gate," Krywonos shouts back.

"Advance!"


**The Gate Opens**

The heavy gate opens with a rusty, grating noise.

The three come to the gate, descend and give the horses' reins to nimble grooms who have been sent to them for this purpose, and enter the besieged city. To prevent them from learning Tulczyn's defensive array and perhaps discovering any weak points, the three are required to wear dark handkerchiefs over their eyes. Thus they are led to the castle.

Inside the shaded castle their blindfolds are removed. A table is set for them, and they sit down before it in pleasure. Refreshments are served. Krywonos expresses his thanks for the hospitality, and takes only a glass of water. Simion licks his swelled lips, and sends an oblique look of inquiry at his commander. For reasons known only to himself, the latter forbids him to eat as he would like to. The priest Dimitri asks no questions, neither by look, voice or hint: silently, he drags over one of the pitchers of wine, pours himself a goblet, and drinks quietly with large, moderate gulps. When he brings the completely dry and empty goblet down from his pale mouth, he wipes his pale lips, which peer out from his thin beard, on the backs of his hands – the left first, then the right for good measure.

"Call for Rabbi Aaron," says Duke Swierszczynski to one of the attendants.

"Halt," says Krywonos, stopping the messenger by grasping the edge of his uniform, and quickly explains: "We don't sit at the same table with a

Jew!"

"They are our allies!," rules the Duke in a voice of affected severity. It is evident that Krywonos' remark has not been rejected outright.

"Either we sit down without Jews, or there'll be no negotiations!" Krywonos pounds on the table with his thick, short-fingered palm. The dishes on the table ring.

The Governor, seated opposite Krywonos, whispers with his two counselors.

"Kazimir," he finally calls to the Officer of the Guard, "go to Rabbi Aaron and explain the situation to him. You may tell him that when the meeting ends he will be informed about every single detail."

Kazimir clicks his high heels, and leaves the hall. The negotiations begin.


## Negotiations

Krywonos argues that it is not proper or fitting for Christian brothers to slaughter each other, saying that even at the start of his attack on Tulczyn he had no intention whatsoever of hurting any good Christian at all, not to mention a Pole who is pious in his religion and faithful to his God and trusts in the Messiah more than any other people, and that his only intention throughout has been to properly slaughter the Jews, the murderers of our God, who, for our manifold iniquities, constitute the majority in the holy city of Tulczyn! Yet the Poles have rashly made an illegitimate pact with them, to protect them with arms and fortifications, and the strength of their hands and their brilliance, leaving his Cossacks no choice except to fight them, for in the heat of battle it is not easy to distinguish who is a Jew and who is a Pole! The Cossacks' proposal: to put an end to this superfluous and silly killing, to remedy the wrong, and to get rid of the Jews once and for all!

"It is obvious," says Krywonos with a cunning smile on his heavy face, "that we should take back from those leeches and return to the rightful owners everything the Jews have sucked and taken through their commerce, which is nothing but robbery in broad daylight and deception, and to divide it among the robbed. In short..." Krywonos sighs, and a queer kind of gravity, like a heavy sadness, troubles his coarse features, which are ugly in any case, and immediately sets Simion sighing too, "let us slaughter the Jews and we will leave you alone, we will retreat from Tulczyn and from all of the Ukraine, we will disappear and never come close to Polish settlements again. We will not have bad memories of you, but only good ones!"

## An Agreement

The priest Dimitri, who during Krywonos' long speech has managed to empty another two goblets of choice wine into his innards, thereby completely emptying the pitcher, nods in affirmation, as if to complement Krywonos' words, which he sees as sacred truth from which there is no escape.

"And the booty?" asks the Governor, with the same affected severity.

"We'll di-vide it!" decrees Krywonos, and once more pounds the table with his heavy hand. It is evident that he is satisfied by the Governor's reaction, and feels like someone whose path has been cleared of all its twistings and its pits have been leveled.

"How?" the Polish Duke asks, not relenting.

Krywonos gives him have a look of astonishment and affront, quite surprising in its frankness: "As is customary between Christian brothers: half for you and half for us!"

The Governor is unsatisfied with Krywonos' answer, and does not accept it. After stubborn and prolonged argument, repeated poundings on the table by the Ataman, and an unequivocal statement that the Cossacks will not agree to less than a third, the Governor falls silent, as a sign that such a division is acceptable to him. Krywonos gets up, offers his hand, which is as red as a steak, to the Governor of Tulczyn, Duke Swierszczynski, and when the latter shakes the outstretched hand, pulls him forcibly to him, hugs him strongly, and declares that the negotiations have come to a successful conclusion.

"Not necessarily," rules the Governor, fixing his hair and his clothes which the hug has disarranged and creased. "We have one more condition, without which this agreement is null and void, and the negotiations will have been fruitless."

"What condition is that?" says Krywonos, staring suspiciously into the Duke's bright eyes, in great tension.

"The agreement shall be recorded, signed by both parties, and reinforced by vow!"

For a moment Krywonos considers his interlocutor's words, and then a malicious greenish flame lights up in his eyes:

"It shall be as His Excellency the Duke of the House of Swierszczynski says!" Krywonos' voice thunders, and he leans forward once more to pull the Pole to his bosom, but the Duke recoils in time, and, with no other option, Krywonos makes do with a handshake.

The contract is recorded and signed. The priest Dimitri, speaking for Krywonos, Simion and himself, articulates an Orthodox vow, in the name of "the Christian Cossack forces," to keep faith according to the signed contract, to slaughter Jews only and not to harm a single Pole, and immediately after the slaughter to evacuate the city of Tulczyn and its environs. The Catholic priest, who not long ago officiated at the Duke's vow to the Jews, repeats the very same vow and the same ceremony with complete seriousness, without skipping even one of its details. Then the Duke commands that the goblets be filled, and together with the members of the deputation empties one goblet after another. For every goblet the Governor drinks, the Cossacks manage to empty three into their innards.

Before the sun sets, the deputation leaves the castle, after having determined the signals and signs which will invite the Cossacks to come inside the fortress's bounds and to slaughter the Jews.

## The Change

As soon as the deputation leaves the fortified city, Tulczyn's Governor, instead of inviting Rabbi Aaron, his Jewish ally, issues an order instructing the Jews to disarm within twenty-four hours.

The Jews on the wall realize in which direction the wind is blowing, and what this order means. They control their fury, and gaze at their Polish friends with amazement and a kind of strange embarrassment, like that of someone who catches a thief and discovers that it is his good neighbor. The Poles try to avoid their gaze.

Wiaczeslaw, Abraham the Blacksmith's friend, cannot bear the deep misery which has spread among the wall's defenders, and decides:

"I'll go and find out what this is all about!" and heads for the castle. An hour later Wiaczeslaw returns. His demeanor is stern, alienated, and he repeats the order, emphasizing that the Jews must report to one of the authority's storehouses and hand over their weapons. All the Jews, without exception!

Abraham looks at the face of his friend of yesterday and the day before, and does not comprehend the change that has occurred in it, or, more correctly, does not believe what his eyes see: of the fierce friendship and the declared loyalty, nothing remains. The Polish officer with the golden curls looks condescendingly at the Jewish blacksmith, his whole demeanor saying "Listen to the order, Jewboy! For, if you don't, your end will be very bitter!"

## The Rabbi's Court

The Jews descend the wall, mournful, shamed, agitated in heart. Instead of returning home to the bosom of their families, they direct their steps to the court of Rabbi Aaron, whom all, Gentiles as well as Jews, honor and respect for his great wisdom and his understanding of the hidden ways of the world, and because he is dauntless, a symbol of purity and honesty.

They pour out before him their bitter words and the pain of their hearts, and tell him about the order that everyone understands what is concealed behind it, and where the negotiations with the Cossacks conducted in the castle have led. If the Rabbi so orders, they will go out to fight against the Polish "ministers," and will overcome them in a matter of hours, thus preventing the fall of Tulczyn and its fortress to the enemy, and saving their own lives, and those of their families. The Jews fall silent, raising their eyes to their rabbi and leader, in immaculate willingness to carry out whatever the latter decides and orders.

### The Ruling of Rabbi Aaron

The chronicler, Rabbi Natan Neta Hannover, quotes the ruling of the *Gaon*, Our Teacher and Master, Rabbi Aaron, leader of the Jews in Tulczyn in those days of distress:

"Hear, my brothers and my people! We are in the Exile among the nations. If you strike at the ministers (the Poles – S.K.), all the kings of Edom (Poles and Russians – S.K.) will hear of it, and, God forbid, will take their revenge on all our brothers in the Exile! Hence, if this is ordained from heaven, we will accept the verdict with joy! We are no better than our brothers in the holy community of Namrov (where all the Jews were slaughtered by that same Krywonos – S.K.), and God may grant us mercy before those who hate Him, perhaps they will take all our precious possessions as ransom for our souls!"

Such are the words of the rabbi and leader of the Jews of Tulczyn, faithfully recorded by Rabbi Natan Hannover, man of many sufferings.

The Jews obey their rabbi, leave his court, and lay down at the feet of the Poles "all their precious possessions," silver, gold and ornaments and, beside them, the weapons they have used adeptly. Then they let the Poles imprison them, while their hearts bleed.

## Ludmilla

The entire matter of the secret-overt agreement becomes known to Ludmilla from the mouth of one of the attendants who was present at the meeting and witnessed the solemn vows that the Poles and the rebelling Cossacks swore to the other. As if taken by a sudden fit, the maiden runs to her father, falls at his feet, firmly refuses to get up from the floor, and tearfully begs him not to carry out this ugly agreement, not to disarm the Jews, but to have mercy on them, and above all, to have mercy on his own good name and his honor, which to this very day has been free of any stain, but which will now be blemished with the blackest of stains, the stain of betrayal.

The Duke fumes at the piercing words of the daughter he loves above all, and can hardly control himself. In a grating voice he tells her that there is and can be no obligation to keep faith with the dirty Jews, who crucified the Messiah and tortured and abused Him, and who in any case are scum, the embodiment of treachery, champions at leading astray, and anyone who abuses them and removes them from the world is a pious man and a keeper of the commandments, and becomes holy to his God. He sees that his one and only daughter, instead of understanding him and standing by him without reservation or protest, wants to rebuke him for his words, the essence of which she fails to understand. He is pained for her before God, and, as a master by his Messiah's commandment, and as the Governor of Tulczyn, he commands her to close herself up at once in the castle, and not to leave it until he commands otherwise, and tells her that she has only one obligation: to obey him!

The maiden Ludmilla, whose beauty can arouse all that is noble in the heart of all who behold it, raises her proud head erect and looks at her father. Astonishment floods her deep, blue eyes. There is a long moment of hesitation, as if the Governor's utterances were being weighed in a sensitive balance, word by word, sentence by sentence. The astonishment makes way for a kind of chill of estranging freedom, something akin to demonstrated contempt, which borders on compassion.

Slowly the maiden rises from the floor, straightens her back, her tears already dry on her cheeks, and rules in a metallic voice, totally strange to herself.

"I will not obey!"

She turns and goes out of the hall like a queen, leaving behind a beaten man, robbed of his power of speech and his ability to change his mind in time.

A minute later the Governor recovers and runs after his daughter. His servants inform him in total submission that the maiden Ludmilla has taken a horse from the stable and galloped off somewhere. Duke Swierszczynski, Tulczyn's Polish governor, yells out like one who has lost his senses:

"Kazimir!"

The burly garrison commander reports to him.

"Take your men and go down to Rabbi Aaron's court. There you will surely find the maiden Ludmilla. Arrest her, by force if necessary, and lock her up in St. Janusz' Tower!"

St. Janusz' Tower rises to a height of some eighteen meters, and at its top is a low monk's cell, with an exit to a narrow landing which surrounds the cell like a balcony with a crumbling parapet. A Polish monk named Janusz, who imposed almost complete isolation upon himself, stayed in that cell until his death, coming out to the tottering balcony only on saints' days and holy days, to bless the crowd gathered at the foot of the tower. Because this crowd grew larger every year, a broad garden was planted at the foot of the tower, and was surrounded by a high wall with an iron gate. It was into this garden that Duke Swierszczynski thought to cram the Jews and then hand them over to their slaughterers, according to the agreement.

### Michael Ben Aaron

Like a tempest, Ludmilla bursts into Rabbi Aaron's home, finding there the one her soul is longing for – Michael, who is kneeling and reciting psalms before going to hand over his arms to the Poles and be imprisoned by them, to be delivered to his murderers.

Ludmilla kneels beside him, kisses the floor at his feet and then his two hands, which she moistens with her tears.

"Flee, love of my soul, flee!" the maiden cries in a stifled voice. "My father has betrayed you, may God forgive him for his weakness! Flee, and do not tarry! If you want," she adds fervently, "I'll join you, I'll come with you, I'll go wherever you go!"

Michael, it seems, is not surprised by the maiden's sudden appearance, or by her agitation.

He is in a kind of state of detachment, a state sometimes entered by those who have decided to do away with themselves.

"No," he answers, softness and light coming from his quiet, sharp-featured face, and penetrating and illuminating her heart. He adds in the same clear voice: "My place is here. A Jew who runs away from the suffering and afflictions meant for him is a deserter!"

His deep glance caresses her hair and her proud head. A happiness which she had not imagined could exist overflows her heart. She falls into his arms and fiercely embraces him.

At that moment the door is kicked open, and, before anyone can utter a word, the guard bursts into the low room. Kazimir calls to Ludmilla and commands her to accompany him, by her father's order. Without understanding what is happening, a stranger to the surroundings and herself, Ludmilla detaches herself from Michael's stalwart hands and goes with the guardsmen.

## St. Janusz' Garden

The Jews have been collected in that broad garden, St. Janusz' Garden, and they kneel in prayer, make supplications and plead for mercy from Heaven. Some weep quietly, while others lament their bitter fate with heart-rending cries.

Krywonos is given the signal: the sign, a red flag easily seen from a distance, is hoisted over Tulczyn's wall. He comes at the head of his huge army, enters the city, and heads for the garden. While doing so, Krywonos orders the commanders of his regiments and companies to climb the walls with their men, and not to let anyone approach them, and also to put a tight guard on the Duke's castle. The Poles are confused, but they have no way of reacting.

And this is the how the slaughter of the Jews by Krywonos' Cossacks is described by the holy rabbi, Natan Neta Hannover:

"And the Greeks (the Cossacks – S.K.) put the Jews under guard in a completely closed garden so that they would not flee, and tarried for a long time. And there were in the place another three *Gaonim* (besides Rabbi Aaron – S.K.): The *Gaon*, Our Teacher and Master Eliezer, The *Gaon*, Our Teacher and Master Shlomo, and The *Gaon*, Our Teacher and Master Chaim. And these three warned the holy people to sanctify the name of Heaven and not to convert to another religion, and they answered as one: 'Hear O Israel, the Lord our God the Lord is One – just as in your hearts He is but One, so in our hearts He is but One.' And it came to pass after these words that there came to them the intermediary, who thrust a flag into the ground and said to them in loud voice: 'He who wants to convert will remain alive, and will live under this flag.' Not one person answered him. He made this announcement thrice, but they made no answer. Thereupon he immediately opened the garden gate, and they all entered in great rage, and killed them in a great massacre, some one thousand and five hundred souls, in all the strange deaths in the world, and the three great rabbis too fell to the sword... And they took ten live rabbis and put iron chains on their feet and placed them under guard till they redeem themselves for ten thousand gold coins, and among these were the *Gaon*, Our Teacher and Master, Rabbi Aaron, son of the *Gaon*, Our Teacher and Master, Rabbi Meir." But Michael, the son of Rabbi Aaron who remained alive, was among the fallen, and slaughtered with him were Abraham the Blacksmith, and the young rabbi, Shlomo, the prodigy, for whom such a great future had been predicted.

Ludmilla sees it all from the tower, and suddenly identifies Michael, who is lying on the fresh grass, bleeding. Her soul fills with an irresistible longing and an unbearable distress, and she kneels, says a short prayer and crosses herself, mounts the parapet of the tottering balcony, and throws herself from the tower onto her beloved, who lies dead on the soft lawn.

Ludmilla falls close to Michael, and her tender body hits the ground. She is probably killed on the spot, but, behold a miracle! Her corpse turns over, and she finds her resting place on Michael's outstretched arm.

On hearing the thud, some of the Cossacks run up to the place, and, seeing what has happened, return to their labor of killing.

Krywonos, who has followed the slaughter most alertly and is pleased with the skill of his men, sees the maiden jump from the tower, hit the ground and roll on, and now approaches, curious. Burly Simion, his deputy, hastens after him.

Krywonos stands over the two bodies, that of the slaughtered man, and that of the young maiden whose perfect beauty death has left unmarred.

The Ataman looks and marvels, touching his tangled beard, and sinks into his thoughts. Simion breaks in, declaring:

"Why this is the daughter of Duke Swierszczynski, or what ever his name is. Let's take her to him, so he can enjoy the sight!"

"Take nothing to that greasy Pole.... Can't you

see – there's love here!" Krywonos stresses the word with a strange kind of softness, completely foreign to him, while pointing at the two bodies.

"May Your Highness order it, and we shall take these two bodies and bury them together, so that they will never be separated again, if it so please Your Highness!" The giant clumsily clicks the heels of his worn-out boots, and salutes his commander in the Polish fashion. Something of the latter's emotions have reached him too.

"So be it!" rules Krywonos, sighs a bitter sigh and, suddenly, commands in his thunderous voice: "Cease!"

The order resounds in the Cossacks' ears, and they obey. All at once they stop the slaughter and return to their commander, cleaning their blood-dripping swords and daggers on the clothes of their victims lying in the garden.

"Your Highness!" cries one of the commanders, a merry young fellow called Styopa, "we have almost finished the work. If you allow us, we will send a few more dirty Jews to their hell!"

"And we'll also find dirty Jews under the piles of corpses, those who played it smart... except that it's no pleasure to burrow there, and the piles are large, and the corpses of the dead are heavy!" remarks a Cossack with a curly mustache that is turning gray, "but, if Your Highness so orders, we shall hear and obey!"

"Enough, I said," Krywonos roars. "Vacaaate the plaaaace!"

The slaughterers leave the garden and lock it behind them. According to Rabbi Hannover's report, they returned to it after three days, calling out: "'Whoever remains alive need not fear, and may stand up, for the sword has already passed over them.' And about three hundred people stood up, those who had fallen amidst the corpses to save themselves, and were now smitten with hunger and thirst, and with many wounds, and they went to that city (Tulczyn – S.K.), aching and weak, tired and barefoot and naked, and the Greek residents of the city (the Cossacks – S.K.) were good to them, and set them free."

Indeed, the Russian is a man of vicissitudes, destined to surprise, and does not know what to expect from himself. Three days before, they had slaughtered the Jews with frothing fury, great anger and wrath, and now, three days later, they cursed themselves for their cruelty, melted in their mercy towards their victims, cried with them and supported them, rescued them from the valley of slaughter, gave them of their bread, dressed them in clothes and put coins in their pockets, and sent them on their way with blessings and sobbings and lamentings straight from the heart. No one who saw the end of this matter would have believed its beginning.

## Krywonos

Krywonos, together with about three dozen of his Cossacks, burst into the castle, and, after removing every Pole bearing a weapon or wearing armor out of his way, found the Duke and Duchess seated for dinner at a round table, being served by two uniformed servants, both registered Cossacks who had turned Catholic.

"Ah! Dinner, Your Excellency the Duke, Panie Swierszczynski!" Krywonos' tone did not bode well.

The Duke's glance scouted about in vain for his guardsmen. They were not visible in any of the alcoves, nor were their steps heard in the corridors.

"Let the Ataman Krywonos please join us, and grace our company. We would consider it a pleasure." The Polish Duke's voice was saturated with servility.

"Brother!" Krywonos' laughter roared in Simion's ears. He began laughing too, and very soon all his entourage was engulfed in wild, rolling, deafening laughter which resounded through all the halls and dark corridors of the castle.

"What did I tell you, Simion?" Krywonos yelled towards his deputy, who bent down to hear his commander's words better. "The Poles are well-mannered! They understand books and science, and wear elegant uniforms! And we, the Cossacks, are boors and idiots in their eyes, dolts to the last generation, incapable of serving them properly! Look at our people," he said, pointing to the servants. "They serve His Excellency the Duke and his *Pani,* the Duchess, and won't even look at us, their brothers and people! They are ashamed of us! Eeeyyachh!"

"I'll talk with them, and they won't be ashamed anymore," suggested Simion. His suggestion set the servants' hearts trembling, and their bodies shivering. One of them almost spilled the soup in the silver casserole he was serving the Duchess from.

"Enough!" shrieked Krywonos, and in his eyes greenish flames of cunning and malice scurried about, with that disgusting pleasure of a predator gloating over its victim, not gobbling it down until it has played with it sufficiently.

"Guards!" called Duke Swierszczynski, his voice and body both trembling. For a moment silence fell on the hall, which was lit with many thick candles giving a sharp light. Krywonos broke the hush:

"Guards!" he cried, mimicking the Duke's cry, and his deliberate, stammered mimicry again aroused the Cossacks crowded at one end of the broad hall to roaring laughter. One of the Cossacks went over to touch the candlestick of a burning candle in the middle of the table.

"Don't fool around, Yepimi!" Krywonos called to him. "Why, you can't even tell the difference between silver and lead, so how will you distinguish between copper and gold – by touch? You're stupid and you'll always be stupid! And this candlestick is pure gold," Krywonos determined. "You can tell even from afar, from the first look. And it is stolen, and so is the second one, and those in the corners. My Lord Duke, the Governor, Panie Swierszczynski..." Krywonos added in derision, and the faces of the Duke and his wife paled, and the Duchess's legs trembled under the table, and the Duke made every effort to control the quiver taking hold of his lower jaw, and succeeded to a degree, "... is a thief!" Krywonos now spoke in a strangely quiet tone, and emphasized his words, with growing pleasure – "A thief like you and me. He bought the candlestick by snatching it from his Jews, whom he executed by our hands!"

The Governor jumped to his feet and drew his

sword.

"What a show," the Ataman Krywonos cried, melting with pleasure. He tried to imitate the way the Governor had jumped up and drawn his sword, and deliberately failed. Once again thunderous laughter flooded the entourage.

*"Niemam pieniadze, mam honor,"* added Krywonos, turning to his deputy. "What do you think, Simion... Oh, I forgot you don't understand Polish. All the better! A foppish language, and all – lies! Even the saying 'I have no money, but I'm honorable' is all deception and leading astray. It is not money that you have, and if you do, it's stolen, and, as to honor, it's the honor of a turkey... ha, ha, ha Simion!"

"Yes, Your Highness!" said Simion, straightening himself theatrically.

"Have you seen what armor this *"pan"* wears under his clothes? Mail armor, which even protects his neck. Do you see?"

"I most certainly do, my commander, Your Highness the Ataman Krywonos!" said Simion, infected by his commander's derisive, enjoyable enthusiasm.

"What do you think? Can my sword overcome this armor, or, will the armor overcome it? What do you think, Simion?" The question was asked in total seriousness, as if the issue was the quality of building material that the Cossack was going to buy to build his house with.

Simion mused, trying to fulfill his role properly, and actually succeeded: "I cannot know, Your Highness," and, pretending to have suddenly had a brilliant idea, went on: "But we could try and carry out an experiment. Why, the noble *"pan"* would not deny a couple of ignorant Cossacks such a small and simple pleasure – to carry out an experiment in order to find out, on the spot, which is the more trusty, the armor or the sword!"

"You're a genius, my Simion!" Krywonos cried, his cry arousing jabberings of amazement among the Cossacks, and support of Simion's proposal. As a sign of appreciation, the Ataman nodded to his deputy, who bent over slightly and kissed his benefactor's hand.

"So, take the lady away, since she has no interest in such experiments," Krywonos ordered. "And we will carry out our experiment, and prove which is better forged, the fine Polish armor, or the steel of my sword, and we'll see if the dirty Jew who sold it to me did not cheat me when he swore that even the finest of steels would not stop its thrust!"

The Duchess tried to resist, and called to her husband, but the Duke understood well where things were heading, and did not respond to her cry, thus helping Simion to carry her past the door. The two converted servants evaporated from the hall as if carried off by the wind.

The Governor turned to Krywonos and, in a soft, fatherly and reconciled voice, remarked:

"You have sworn faithfulness by all that is holy to you and by your God, and you have kissed the cross, and have taken upon yourselves every curse if you break your agreement...."

"We learn from you," answered Krywonos in a grim and serious voice which would brook no comments. "You swore by everything holy to you, and by your God, and you kissed the cross, and took upon yourselves every curse if you betrayed the Jews, and you surely betrayed them! We are the messengers of your God, we bring down on your heads what you deserve!"

Krywonos approached the tall, heavy Pole, who was dressed in elegant clothes, under which, indeed, gleamed his mail armor, which protects even the throat and neck of the person who wears it.

The Governor of Tulczyn threw his heavy sword away from himself. The sword rolled and fell at Krywonos' feet, dragging dishes from the set table along with it. The dishes scattered over the floor, with a sad sound.

"Strike an unarmed man, if that is your honor!" Duke Swierszczynski called out.

"Honor I leave for you and your kind!" said Krywonos and, after removing the table which separated them, he shouted: "This is what you deserve!" With a single swing of the sword he severed the handsome head, which had once been proud but at the moment of death was beset by fear, and the fear was not concealed.

Loud laughter washed over the hall. Simion, back from his mission, yelled out loudly:

"The dirty Jew didn't lie, even though he was a dirty Jew!"

## Conclusion

And these are the words of the wise and holy rabbi, Natan Neta Hannover, of blessed memory: "After killing the Jews, they approached the fortress to fight, and the ministers said to them: 'Did you not make a pact with us, and why do you violate your covenant?' And the Greeks (the Cossacks – S.K.) said to the ministers: 'As you did to the Jews, violating your covenant, so shall we do to you, measure for measure!' And the Greeks acted cunningly, and burned the fortress to the ground, and killed all the ministers, a great killing, and took their property as booty, and as for the Duke (Swierszczynski – S.K), before his death they tortured his wife and his two daughters before his eyes. And he was a very big man, and he sat on the chair and could not rise. And they cut off his head... cruelly... And all the ministers (the Poles – S.K.) who heard of this justified the judgment of Heaven on them, and from that day forth the ministers strengthened the hands of the Jews, and did not hand them over to the criminals, and even though the Greeks swore to them a number of times that they would not do anything to the ministers, but only to the Jews, they did not believe then any more. Were it not for this, Israel would not have had a surviving remnant, God forbid."

Truly, Rabbi Aaron had been right, had ruled wisely, and had foreseen the outcome. His flock had obeyed him, and in their sufferings and their deaths had redeemed their brothers, the Children of Israel, throughout the Christian world, and had fittingly and properly fulfilled the verse which says "All of Israel are warranty for one another." They acted like their fathers before them, and like their children and grandchildren in the generations to come.

# IVAN NOVOTNY

## The Cornerstone

According to unsubstantiated studies, the savage tribes which appeared in Europe between the ninth and sixth centuries B.C.E. are the cornerstone of the German nation and the forefathers of the Teutonic people.

The language of the Germans is the language of Goethe and Schiller, and of the Jew Heinrich Heine. Charles V, who set his mind on greatness, conquered the lion's share of Europe, and tried to unite all the Christian peoples under his scepter, boasted to his courtiers that he understood German, and even talked German –with his horses.

Environment, food and drink are mentioned as being among the factors which contribute to the building of the noble characteristics of peoples and nations.

The environment, known for its glory and splendor, in which the German people grew and developed, is – the forest. As for its food and drink, the German people leaves little room for doubts and reflections: tubers, lard, and pork are its nutrients, and beer, not the choicest, is its national drink.

A forest, potatoes, pork, lard, and beer – and what is the result? In his masterpiece *The Magic*

*Mountain,* Thomas Mann, Nobel Laureate for Literature, gives a quite exhaustive definition of his brothers, the Germans:

"Anyone who does not serve the best and most expensive wines with his meals has no one to dine with, and his daughters wither in their virginity. That is the way of people, and that is their nature. As I lie here (in a Swiss sanatorium – S.K.) and look on from afar, I see it in all its coarseness... indifference and – ? and firmness! Yes, but what does it mean? It means: harshness, chilliness. And what do harshness and chilliness mean? They mean cruelty... unappeasable cruelty. When one lies here and looks on from afar, one is seized with shuddering."

### The Open Secret

The genealogical tree of , the "Fuehrer," whom the Germans revered, adored and worshipped as a god, and did all they could to implement his theory, the theory of the master race, is embarrassingly simple and inescapably clear.

The, naked, dry, well-known and substantiated facts are:

"Hitler's father was the illegitimate son of a woman named Schickelgruber, from Lending, near Linz, who was employed as a cook at a household in Graz. The cook Schickelgruber, Hitler's grandmother, worked for a Jewish family named Frankenberger when she became pregnant and bore her child. At that time, in the thirties of the 19th century, Frankenberger (the Jew – S.K.) in the name of his son, who was then about nineteen, paid Schickelgruber a paternity allowance from the date of her son's birth till his fourteenth year. There was also correspondence between the Frankenbergers and Hitler's grandmother, the general sense of which indicates the correspondents' unstated knowledge that Schickelgruber had become pregnant in circumstances which obliged Frankenberger to pay a paternity allowance" *(The Face of the Third Reich,* by Joachim Fest).

In the opinion of other researchers, the Frankenbergers paid Mrs. Schickelgruber a paternity allowance until her illegitimate son, Alois, the father and progenitor of Adolf Hitler, grew up and obtained a post.

A person with such an open and simple genealogical tree would not have been accepted by the Nazi Party under its declared constitution, and the criteria there practiced. Moreover, that constitution and the Nuremberg Racial Purity Laws would have sent that same person immediately and without hesitation to the Nazi extermination camps.

Adolf Hitler – the corporal who won the Iron Cross First Class in the World War I, the failed painter, the high-school student who was kept back in the same class twice and who did not conclude his studies, the sworn vegetarian – never spoke about himself. That, at any rate, is the testimony of his researchers and acquaintances.

"These people do not have to know who I am," he said nervously to his nephew, William Patrick Hitler, "nor where or what my family comes from" (*Der Spiegel,* no. 31, 1967).

And he started an unforgettable and uncompromising, cold, calculated, monstrous and merciless holy war of destruction against his grandmother's seducer, demanding nothing less than to annihilate him from the world, to exterminate him completely, to wipe his memory from the face of the earth, and to cleanse it of his blood, which – so it turns out – flowed in his own veins and comprised at least 25% of his own blood.


## The Hunt

The Germans hated the Jews with a clean and orderly German hatred, anchored in law and defined scientifically. They created an innovation in the formulation of the reasons and arguments for hating Jews, adding a new element: the Jews are persecuted also because they are a people of seducers.

The ugly males of that notorious tribe, with their long hooked noses, their blood which is mixed with Negro blood, and their crooked legs, seduce the pure and chaste Teutonic girls, brutally desecrating their honor.

It may be that the innovation was not extremely original, but now, for the first time, it was articulated in pure German, and set out in an unequivocal official communique.

In the Second World War the German tanks tore across the soil of Poland, defeating this country in less than three weeks. In their scientific way, which is based on clear rules and unequivocal laws, the Germans started a persistent hunt for the "seducers" and, with the active and enthusiastic help of the local population, imprisoned them in the Warsaw Ghetto, from where, according to Teutonic order, they were to be sent to the ovens, and to become choice organic fertilizer and all-purpose soap.

## Jacob Lipschitz

Jacob Lipschitz was fourteen when his parents were forced to abandon their spacious apartment on Rybaki Street, not far from the Gdansk Pier, and move into a narrow room with shared toilet and kitchen and no shower, on Zamenhof Street, in the Ghetto. This room was allotted to them after harsh and prolonged negotiations, which all centered around how many grams of gold were to be given to a handsome Judenrat official who was active in the sphere of housing.

Day and night Mrs. Lipschitz, Jacob's young mother, cried and lamented bitterly as she sat in that narrow, unventilated room, but to no avail. Jacob's father, Aaron Lipschitz, a solid, middle-aged man, formerly a respectable textile merchant, tried to console his wife by proving to her, with examples and signs, that the German people, in the end, are a cultured people, and that the present situation was only temporary, just a brief interlude, an instant compared with the grave events of history, and everybody would come to their senses, and everything would return to normal and be as it was. For a long time the wife refused to believe him, but she finally gave in and, apparently, was consoled and started getting involved in life in the Ghetto, which was cut off from all reality.

In retrospect, it turned out that Aaron Lipschitz' words of consolation regarding the temporary nature of this "brief" period were something of a prophesy, and were fulfilled, literally and profoundly, but in complete contradiction to the explicit intention of their pronouncer: about a year and a half after their arrival in the Ghetto, the Lipschitz couple was taken from their place of work at a mattress factory, and transported to the "Treblinka" extermination camp, from which they never returned.

From that day on, Jacob became the sole owner of that unventilated room on Zamenhof Street.... His parents had used to obtain some extra bread or potatoes in addition to the hundred grams of bran bread the Ghetto inmates received, for money, which they still had, as well as gold or jewelry. He turned the room upside down, but did not find a single coin or piece of jewelry. His parents must have carried their treasure on their own bodies. So, with regard to food, his situation got worse and worse. He didn't give up. He started going with the bands of youngsters of his own age that roamed the streets, and knew that they sometimes went outside the Ghetto by secret ways and got hold of bread and potatoes, and occasionally even cheese and butter. They did not consent to reveal their secret to him, and he understood them. Any Jew who left the Ghetto and got caught, or was informed on, would be executed by hanging or shooting, or in any other way.


## The Poet

Before the Germans came, Jacob Lipschitz was a pupil at the St. Stanislaw School, a mixed school. He was not an excellent pupil, but he was highly praised for the poetic talent he displayed. He rhymed stirring lines in pure Polish that embarrassed the literature teacher to the point where she had to admit that even a Pole by birth could not easily attain the level of language mastery of her thirteen-year-old Jewish pupil. He also had a schoolmate, Alexandra Lebowa, whose Polish blood was mixed with Russian blood, who would turn pale on hearing the poems of Jacob, the dark Jewish boy, and would do everything she could to get close to him. More than once, during a lesson, she passed him a fresh flower she had picked in some yard, and her gaze, fixed on his eyes in wonderment, never hid her adoration and even something a thousand times more than that.

They became friends, and used to go out to the spacious Krasinski Garden. They would find a quiet corner on the bank of the Vistula, and Jacob would read his short, lyric poems to Saszenka – Alexandra – and she would listen with love and awe, to the point of complete disassociation from her surroundings. She would finally sigh, pass a deep, caressing gaze over his face, and make a statement which no one would dispute, that a poet the likes of Jacob Lipschitz had never before appeared in Poland, nor would such a one easily appear. And she would add that every line that he read to her made her heart overflow with the thrill of a strange freedom. At one of their meetings, Saszenka made him a present of a moist and bashful kiss on the cheek.

Then came the war, and the Germans, and the Nuremberg Laws. The Jews were forced to leave their apartments in the "Aryan" neighborhoods of Warsaw, and to crowd into the "Ghetto," a prison surrounded by a wall, eighteen kilometers in length and three meters high, its broad upper edge strewn with broken glass. The Jews' link with the outside world was severed, as was that between Jacob and Saszenka.

## Fritz

The bands of youngsters used to sit on the sidewalk in silence. This silence stemmed, among other things, from the exhaustion caused by hunger. Jacob got used to it, and finally accepted it as something to be taken for granted, and did not hasten to violate it.

One day, a tall, corpulent German, with a beet-red face and tiny eyes covered by steel-framed glasses, appeared at the end of the street. A smile was spread on his twisted lips, and his appearance made an impression of bumbling ludicrousness tending towards friendliness. He tried to prove this. "What are you so dejected for?" he called out to them in German, which a considerable number of the youngsters had learned to understand. "That's not the way of youngsters! Let's play a game!" From close up he looked younger and more energetic.

"Do you have a ball?" His voice was high and awkward.

There was no ball.

"If you don't have a ball," called the German, "let's box. All of you against me! Come on, I don't want to harm you, just to get some exercise!"

He spoke sincerely.

Several of the boys paid for the "harmless"

boxing with broken teeth and "black eyes", and one got a broken nose, which bled for a long time. Each time Fritz lifted his heavy fists to him, Jacob Lipschitz quickly fell flat on the ground, acknowledging his opponent's undisputed victory. The latter was pleased.

"What's your name, dirty Jew?" Fritz asked when the game was over.

"Jacob," he answered, adding "I'm not a 'dirty Jew'!"

"Ha, ha, ha, ha!," the German burst out in coarse, uncontrolled laughter, strange flames of undefined, embarrassing satisfaction glinting in his shortsighted eyes. "So what are you if you're not a dirty Jew?"

"A Jew," answered Jacob Lipschitz, as if taking part in a game, but not giving up his position.

"All right!" the German concluded derisively. "Be a Jew! And you see," he said, turning to the aching group of youngsters, who were afraid to disband, "this Jacob, he's the smartest of you all. He's a 'Jew,' and not a 'dirty Jew!' And all the rest of you are – dirty Jews! Without exception! Bring any sort of ball tomorrow, so we can have some exercise!"

This Fritz became real trouble. They brought a homemade ball of rags, but it did not satisfy him, and he returned to the boxing, and was no longer pleased by the falls of surrender now adopted by the whole band. His blows were heavy, and the bruises were many. There was no escape other than getting away before the fight and hiding from him. He would be hurt and insulted, and on one of his visits he took out his pistol and fired a number of shots towards the silent windows of the houses, crying:

*"Raus, schmutzige Juden!"* ("Out, dirty Jews!"). Come out and we'll have a competition! Bring a ball, and, if not, get your fists ready!"

But the *"schmutzige Juden"* refused to answer and come out, and avoided Fritz like the plague.


## Zbydenie

As already stated, Jacob knew that among his acquaintances of his own age were some who knew how to get out of the Ghetto one way or another to obtain food. They, the "foray men," or "foray boys," as they were called by the Ghetto residents, could be easily recognized: their faces still retained some gleam, at times even a roundness, and their eyes projected a smartness and alertness, unlike the dull gaze of the rest.

His schoolmate, Zbydenie – whose parents were completely assimilated and had not even circumcised their son, and had given him a proper Polish name, Zbydenie, rather than Eliahu, Aaron or Jacob, as his own parents had called him, but had been transported to their death, just like his parents – undoubtedly belonged to the "foray boys." Once Zbydenie had needed his help in geometry, especially in descriptive geometry, which requires a clear imagination anchored in logic. Would he remember the help he had generously given him?... And, if Zbydenie should actually consent to reveal the secret passage to him, and he could get beyond the walls, whom would he turn to? The answer to his pointed question appeared in his brain with an easy, somewhat embarrassing clarity: to Saszenka....

## The Passage

He found an opportunity to have a brief talk with the elusive Zbydenie:

"I'm willing to risk my life, if only to get out!" He knew that Zbydenie did not require clarifications such as "where to" or "where from".

Without answering his gaze, Zbydenie said curtly:

"And what will be my reward?"

"Heartfelt thanks!"

"And if you're caught?"

"I won't betray you!"

A long, scrutinizing gaze, surprising in its maturity and wise tranquil strength.

The eyes look down again. The scrutiny and questioning are not to his detriment. Zbydenie takes the identifying armband off his arm, stuffs it into one of the pockets of his threadbare trousers, quietly faces about, and, with a quick step, heads eastward. Jacob rapidly does the same: he removes the armband from his arm and stuffs it in his pocket, and hurries to catch up to Zbydenie. It is not easy for him to keep up with his friend's brisk pace.

They leave the last houses of the Ghetto. Jacob is breathing heavily. Zbydenie turns left, goes around a high, disintegrating wall, and disappears from his field of vision.

Jacob steps carefully. Dense, wild-growing gladioli, thorns the height of a man, a dry bush. And, behind them – a dark opening, leading, so it seems, into the depths of the earth. He descends into it. A sewage canal. The smell is heavy. He feels a weakness, but recovers, and goes on walking.

Suddenly, a bright light filters in from somewhere, and the air is light and fresh.

## The Outside

His heart is pounding. He ascends cautiously, and emerges through the narrow, filthy opening, walks around a thick bush and turns. The Ghetto wall is behind him.

He engraves the location in his memory. A one-way alley, named Berezanska.

To Saszenka's house it is about a quarter hour of brisk walking. His feet are light. All around him are the other people, the "Aryans," who are free to some extent. He does everything he can not to attract attention. It seems he is succeeding. He keeps walking on, at a measured but brisk pace. A noisy boulevard. He keeps his gaze fixed on the points of his shoes. Right, left, right. Will his heart withstand the tremendous tension? Keep pace and focus on it. While desperately trying to show confidence.

He feels each passing glance at his worn-out clothes. Looks of distraction. People are not interested in him. They have enough with their own distress. But he knows he looks different. In dress as in appearance. And, probably, in expression. Expression identifies better than any yellow armband, Shield of David or inscription of *Jude*. The recoiling expression of a hunted animal, these last two thousand years. Someone might get suspicious. Will he get into trouble because of an informer? Here is the low, square house belonging to Saszenka's parents. He stands before the door. What awaits him on the other side? Saszenka, her parents, or a new tenant, perhaps a German? Once he had been introduced to Saszenka's parents. Congenial people. Have they changed? Has the war made them feverish?

Should he turn back, run, go back the way he came, before it's too late?

He raises his arm and his fist comes down with restraint on the door panel. Once, twice, three times. He can feels his sweat concentrating and coming out of every pore of his body. Separate drops which quickly connect with each other and move like wet fingers over his skin. It's too late to retreat. Behind the door he hears footsteps. Let his fate bring upon him what is decreed for him.

Without making a sound, slowly and carefully, the door retreats before him. In its frame stands a young girl. Saszenka. She hasn't changed at all. Her look, at the first moment, grows darker and darker, and, it seems she is about to collapse at his feet in a faint... He steps toward her, extends his arms, she regains her composure, a smile broadens on her lips and lights up her delicate face. Saszenka!

## Saszenka

Without uttering a word, she takes his hand and leads him to a small yard behind the house, with a high fence which a stranger's eye cannot penetrate. Her hand, which holds his, is trembling. She turns to him, and, as in the past, looks into his eyes with a profound gaze, in which the adoration has given way to pain. Her eyes are moist.

"Jacob!" she says, and he hears his own eager voice, whispering:

"Bread!"

Everything happens in the wildest manner. She runs into the house and brings bread, some pastries, fresh cheese and some other food, and a jug of water.

He chews for a long time. The cookies he stuffs into his pockets. She follows all his movements, and cries. He pays her no attention. He hasn't finished eating yet.

He recalls two youngsters who went outside the Ghetto and brought some jewelry to the goldsmith, who said he would pay them a very small sum, perhaps a hundredth of its value. Instead of that, he went and turned them over to a Polish policeman stationed near the shop. The boys were hung in the Ghetto square, not far from the Judenrat building. For all to see and be afraid.

All saw, but no one was afraid.

Saszenka talks little, in whispers. It turns out that her mother is due to return at any moment. It's not desirable that she meet Jacob. It'd be better that they make dates for future meetings. On safe days, when Saszenka's parents aren't at home. She will wait for him. On Mondays and Wednesdays. Between nine in the morning and one in the afternoon. She will wait. In any case, she has nowhere to go. She also doesn't want to go anywhere. On those days and between those hours he will always find her at home.

Saszenka checks to see if the road is clear. They part in front of the door with a firm hand-shake. At the last moment, she plants a kiss on his cheek, withdraws, and stands in the frame of the open door, waving her white hand. He turns towards her before disappearing at the corner, for a final wave.

### "Fangt Ihn!"

He hurries. And remains cautious. Everything looks all right. The cookies swell his pants pockets. For the first time in about two years he is sated. Full of strength. And another strange phenomenon – his heart is overflowing with happiness and pity. Happiness because the world is so beautiful and generous, and pity that only a few feel like him. Were it possible, he would be willing to divide himself among these grim-looking people, to share his happiness and joy with them. The world is good, and there is no doubt that this is how God created it.

As he crosses the wide boulevard, where the bustle and the crowds have increased at this time of day, he senses, without locating it, a gaze which shakes every capillary of his being. He raises his head and looks cautiously behind him, without stopping. A few buildings away stands the bespectacled Fritz, who seems to be rooted to the spot, totally astounded and insulted.

From that moment on, all his actions are not his own, but those of some other youngster, a complete stranger to him, whom he could observe from the side, or from above, without identifying with him. This youngster was all instinct, not yet defined, like a coiled spring that has been wound up and now activates all the parts it controls with a stormy power.

He runs. And knows that Fritz is running after him. He also grasps, with relief, that the distance between them is increasing. The heavy Fritz, of the master race, chases the young Jacob, of the inferior race. It is as clear from the start how the chase will end. The nimble Jacob will escape the clumsy Fritz, in spite of the Racial Laws.

He dodges his pursuer in the winding alleys, which he knows well, and disappears from his sight at the same moment when the latter yells out in heavy Swabian:

"Catch him!" *"Fangt ihn!"* "Stop!" "Halt!"

No one responds to the call. Jacob Lipschitz gives thanks for the degree of indifference that characterizes large crowds of people, which is considered, not always correctly, to be a destructive element.

Before evening comes, and with it the darkness, Jacob Lipschitz crosses the passage under the eastern wall, and quickly finds a hiding place in one of the dark cellars in the Ghetto, one that is empty of objects or people.

Two days later, as he is walking innocently on Zamenhof Street, he feels a thick arm suddenly clutch his own arm, almost lifting him from the ground and up into the air.

A red face, breathing hard from the unusual excitement, bends over him. Tiny eyes, bespectacled, wicked, challenging, and at the same time proclaiming victory, stare into his own.

"No one escapes Fritz!" he hears the Swabian-German words beat against his ears.

## The Silver-Haired Officer

He is brought to the headquarters.

Fritz clicks his heels and salutes the duty officer, a middle-aged man whose temples have begun to turn silver, with a slight limp in his left foot.

"My Commander!" Fritz cries in a deafening voice, as he salutes. Without turning to the saluting private, the officer nods his head as a sign that Fritz may speak.

Fritz starts to speak to the back of the duty officer, who is bending over his documents and leafing through them with a coldness that bodes no good, and reports how two days ago he saw this *schmutzige Jude* outside of the Ghetto and its wall, and how he chased him, and how the youngster, with distinct Semitic cunning, got away from him, and how he, Fritz, waited for him with patience and set a trap for him, not desisting until he had hooked the fat fish. And here he is, before you. And he, Fritz Schwartzenberger, is ready to be his executioner. An additional click of the heels and a salute, while stretching his corpulent body, signals that the story has been concluded.

The officer turns slowly to his soldier. His elongated face expresses disgust. Jacob understands that the disgust has been aroused not by him, but by his captor, and his heart starts beating again.

Without looking at the soldier, the duty officer asks the boy: "What have you to say in your defense?"

"I have never left the Ghetto!" he cries, his voice trembling.

The officer turns to the private, and asks him:

"When was the last time you visited an optometrist?"

For a long moment Fritz is silent. His tiny eyes run around behind his thick glasses like mice in a trap. Once again he stretches his fat body, clicks his heels, and answers:

"Before the war, *mein Fuehrer!*"

With the same look of disgust the silver-haired officer rules:

"Go for a check-up. You need to add a few diopters. And release the boy!" He turns his broad, somewhat bent back to them both, and goes back to leafing through his papers.

A heel-click, a salute, an about-face, and Fritz takes Jacob outside. Before he lets him go, as commanded, he gives him a prolonged look of hatred and helplessness, bends over him, and spits out in a low voice:

"That officer is leaving tomorrow. From tomorrow on, you're mine!" He takes a shiny, well-oiled revolver out of its holster, and states:

"This is a nine-millimeter Walther!" He extracts the magazine, takes out a bullet, bends over the boy, and, turning the bullet in front of his eyes, whispers as if sharing a secret: "This bullet is reserved for you!" Fritz opens his upper pocket, drops the bullet into it, buttons it up carefully, and lets the boy go.

## Sewer Rat

Jacob Lipschitz continued to make "forays" outside the Ghetto and the wall, to the "Aryan" side of occupied Warsaw, and to meet Saszenka on safe days, at the set times. The portions of food the girl gave him grew larger with time and became more diversified, and he started hoarding what he could for "black days," as people say. And these arrived sooner than he expected. On one of his "forays," which he had become expert at, slipping like a shadow through the city's streets and vanishing among its crowds, the door of Saszenka's house opened with a fierce thrust, and, in its frame stood a tall Pole, Saszenka's father, furious and fuming.

He instinctively retreated and bent down, like someone expecting a blow. He heard the thundering voice of the Pole, who was evidently hurt to the depths of his soul, and saw the lightning shooting from his eyes:

"Get out of here, Jewboy! Out! And never dare to show your dirty face here again! You have endangered the entire family. You have no conscience! No more Saszenka!" The man stopped talking, and bubbles of white froth showed between his lips. It was clear that he was about to slam the door in the face of the uninvited guest.

Here, it appears, Jacob Lipschitz woke up, and without giving consideration to the man's fury and wrath, he stopped the door with his foot and hand, and asked:

"What do you mean 'No more Saszenka?'" An irresistible firmness saturated his voice, his eyes darkened, and it was clear that no force in the world would budge him from here before he had his satisfaction, that is, before his question was answered. And the answer was not slow to come.

"She has been sent to the country! You have contaminated her pure soul, you Jewish sewer rat. Get on, go!"

Jacob retreated, and the door was slammed with such great force that it almost came off its hinges. And he never saw Saszenka's father again.

## "Where is Jacob?"

The source of his food was gone. From his forays Jacob had learned to be wary of people, to sense approaching danger from a distance, and to escape it in the most suitable way, and in good time. By dint of these two capabilities, he evaded the Germans in the two large *"Akzionen"* which descended upon the Ghetto and considerably diluted its population. He burrowed in abandoned buildings and among other things found a little food which had begun to spawn maggots, and several gold coins, which he quickly and easily exchanged for bread and cheese.

Fritz would occasionally appear on Zamenhof Street, walking back and forth and calling out in his dull voice under the broken windows of the houses:

"Where is Jacob, the dirty Jew, where is he?" Then he would laugh, a crushed, hueless laugh. When he succeeded in catching one of the boys, he would place the barrel of his revolver to his temple, and demanded that he immediately reveal the hideout of Jacob Lipschitz, the "dirty Jew." The trapped boy would fall at his feet, and, crying bitterly, swear by all that was dear to him that he knew nothing about "Jacob, the dirty Jew," and didn't even know who he was. The groveling flattered the Swabian. His beet-red face would take on the expression of a fatted animal which has eaten its fill, and he would replace the revolver into its holster and explain, almost in friendliness:

"It would be a shame to waste a choice German bullet on a Jewish mouse like you!" Then he would bend over and tug his victim's ear, until he almost pulled it off, and its owner would scream in pain to high heaven and writhe on the ground for a long time after the German had let him go.

## The Underground

On one of Fritz' rounds, while Jacob was burrowing in a deserted room, his broken cry reached Jacob's ears: "Where is Jacob, the dirty Jew?" He looked through the broken window, and saw him at his pranks.

Fritz was putting the barrel of his revolver to the temple of a lad whose jacket, which reached to his knees, hung on him as on a scarecrow.

"If you don't tell me where Jacob the dirty Jew is" threatened the German, "you'll get the bullet instead of him!"

There was a new, diabolical tone in the German's voice. And it was no longer possible to know to what extent his threat was an idle one, and if he would indeed go back on it, and not pull the trigger.

"Not a dirty Jew, but a Jew," Jacob called out loudly in the direction of the man with the revolver.

Fritz released his victim, lifted his bespectacled eyes in the direction he had heard the voice from, and also raised his revolver.

"Not a Jew, but a 'dirty Jew'!" he insisted.

"Not a 'dirty Jew,' but a Jew" insisted Jacob.

"Your time has come!" frothed Fritz, hurrying to the building from which the boy's voice had burst forth. He climbed the stairs, broke into Jacob's hiding place, but found it empty. The lad had managed to climb onto the roof and escape.

The above event, to which – so it turns out – there had been witnesses, reached the ears of the leaders of the Jewish underground which had been formed in the Ghetto in those days, and aroused much interest. After brief deliberation at the underground headquarters, it was decided to offer Jacob Lipschitz membership in its ranks. He did not refuse, and was attached to Zacharish's section, which belonged to the Dror Hechalutz movement. Zacharish's men were based in Nalewki Street, not far from the organization's headquarters, and from Mardek's group, who were also based in the same street, at number thirty-seven.

The sixteen-year-old Jacob Lipschitz was trained to fire a revolver and a rifle, and to throw home-made incendiary bombs. Like all the underground fighters, he received a modest food supplement, so that his strength would not dwindle beyond a reasonable point.

### Monday, January 18, 1943

On Monday, the eighteenth of January, nineteen hundred and forty-three, the first clash between the Jewish fighting force in the Ghetto and the oppressive forces, which were comprised of Germans, Poles and Ukrainians, occurred. This is how it was described by an eye-witness:

"German Army units besieged the Ghetto from all sides. S.S. men and Ukrainian gendarmes immediately appeared in the streets, and dispersed to every corner. Those Jewish sections which had prepared themselves for work were arrested immediately and brought to the *Umschlagplatz* (the loading square), and anyone who did not manage to find shelter was snatched from the streets. Anyone suspected of trying to escape was shot on the spot. The first victims fell... The *Akzion* was in full swing... The Jewish hospital was emptied. Those patients who had a little strength dragged themselves to the *'Umschlag,'* and those who failed were killed on the spot.

"The rattling noise of the rifles and machine guns drowned the voices of the Jews who were calling for life while being dragged to death by force. The howling of children and the groans of the old. On the road the dead and dying wallowed in their own blood. The dying lifted their eyes to the people marching in line, as if they could help them in their trouble. The marching people perhaps envy those lying there, who are already exempt from the long road of afflictions that leads from the *'Umschlag'* to Treblinka...

"However, after the street hunt, the Germans were forced to go from door to door in order to find those still hiding. Now they discovered that these last Jews were different, and that now their own lives were in danger too.

"In the 'Dror' group at 58 Zamenhof Street they had been preparing all this time for the clash with the enemy. On the third floor a group of forty gathered, and were joined by a number of 'Gordonia' members. We had four pistols and three grenades. The other comrades armed themselves with iron bars, clubs, bottles, and so on. We dispersed to our positions. Even though we knew that this clash would end in our defeat, we were not perplexed: 'We shall fall in battle!' From the window we watched a group of Jews being led to the *'Umschlag.'* Almost automatically, the comrades were summoned to the windows... When the column passed the corner of Zamenhof and Niska Streets, 'Hashomer Hatzair' members dropped grenades on the German escort and on the S.S. men... Some of them fell immediately, some dispersed to find shelter, and the entire column of Jews scattered in every direction. The fighters set up a barricade in a small house in Niska Street, and here they made a stand against the German reinforcements which arrived later. The Germans, unable to make a path into the house, burned it down. All the comrades fired until the last bullet – and fell in battle!"

A Jew who has not lived in the Nazi period, under Nazi rule, or come into contact with the S.S. and the *"Wehrmacht,"* will never be able to understand the full depth and exceptional meaning of the above event. The German, who by dint of the atmosphere of oppression, had seemed to be as made of a different material, diabolical indeed, but invulnerable, who came only to murder and give commands, had suffered a mortal blow, fled in panic, fallen in the street and been killed! The myth had been smashed, a change had occurred in the laws of the universe, the eyes of those blind from birth were opened, to see the abundance of the enchanted light of freedom, which until that very moment he did not know existed.

## "Bunker"

Immediately after the incident which gladdened the hearts of the Jews imprisoned in the Ghetto, the underground feverishly began preparing itself for the inevitable decisive encounter. The key word, or perhaps, the magic word, in those days was – "bunker."

From the end of January until the end of March all the Jews in the Ghetto dug continuously, turning the entire area into a web of sophisticated burrows, the work being carried out at night alone, sometimes by moonlight, sometimes by starlight, and sometimes under a blanket of complete darkness.

The historian Israel Gutman, who took part in these events, writes in his book *The Revolt of the Besieged*:

"Much work and invention were invested in the installation and equipping of the bunkers. Special attention was devoted to hiding the bunker entrances. Almost every bunker used an original invention. In one place, entry was made by moving the boards in the floor above the bunker. Another bunker was accessed only through a narrow chimney. A third entrance was through a hole that was revealed after moving a toilet seat. In the large bunkers, which were shared by tens of families, several openings were made, on the assumption that the place also required an emergency exit. Sophisticated bunkers were equipped with a channel that led into no-man's-land, with here and there an exit on the Aryan side. They were afraid that the Nazis might disconnect the water and electricity lines leading to the Ghetto. Therefore some Jews cleverly connected the bunkers to the main electricity lines and to the main water pipes in the Polish streets."

## Spring

Spring comes early to Warsaw. Deep skies, white clouds, clear mornings, a glad sun.

Jacob Lipschitz breathes deeply of the air before the calamity. The air is clear, light and intoxicating like young wine. Even the stench of the corpses still strewn in the Ghetto's alleys cannot overpower that fine fragrance of renewal and hope. He has an urge to write a poem. Jacob Lipschitz resolutely imprisons this urge. Deep in his pants pocket, which was sewn by an expert tailor, a member of the underground, is a "Parabellum" revolver, his personal weapon. The spring of nineteen forty-three in Warsaw is not the time for lyric outpourings. And Jacob Lipschitz is a lyric poet. He will never adapt to the harsh rhythms of marches. And this spring, in spite of its virginal softness, its magical touch, its gentle fragrance and its intoxicating air, only longs for drums and bugles.

March twenty-second, nineteen forty-three. The first day of spring, in a world enveloped in death, marching to destruction. No, he will not succumb to temptation. He will not write a poem, will not make a rhyme. His hand strokes the cold barrel of the revolver. Nine bullets in the magazine.

Everything is ready. The Jewish fighting organization has cast fear over all the Jewish institutions, over the overt and hidden collaborators, and, indirectly, over the Germans. A leaflet calling on the Jewish workers not to obey the Germans has been distributed. The Germans have responded – not with shooting, arrests and executions, but, how awful! with a leaflet of their own, in which they address the Jews and state unequivocally that the underground is misleading them, and that the German institutions are the only ones which ensure their well-being, their income and their security. And if the underground has a sense of justice and a degree of integrity and courage, the Germans are willing to conduct negotiations with its representatives. Indeed, the Germans are groping in the dark.

### A New Spirit

A new spirit is abroad in the Ghetto. Mordechai Anielewicz, one of the senior commanders of the underground, and, some say, its glorious leader, writes:

"A few days ago... I spoke to a man, just a man from the street, not one of us. I started to get him talking:

"'How are things?' (The writer answers the man he spoke to – S.K.) 'Terrible, my friend! Another *Akzion* in Cracow, one in the Lublin area, so it will be upon us soon...and that will be the end....'

"'What end, sir?' the man asks. 'What happened before won't happen any more. They won't take us like cattle to slaughter any more.'

"'Oh, this is something new,' I thought to myself. And I went on: 'Today you're a hero. But that's nothing. Tell me, what would you do if they came to take you away?

"'What do you mean, what would I do? Then there would be no need for any propaganda. I would gather all my friends, we would take up axes, iron bars, and hammers, and go down to the cellars, or barricade ourselves in our apartments. Let them come! Let them be pounded right and left by machine guns. What will they do to me when I'm hidden behind my door? And, if one of them sticks his head into the room, he's mine. Ten will fall from my axe. I might be the eleventh. But that, at least, is a good way to die. No, no, they won't take me like before. And for them, for the Jewish policemen, see what I've prepared.' He showed me a long, strong, well-sharpened knife. 'God help anyone who starts with me!'"

The underground levies taxes, judges offenders, catches and executes traitors. Will the Germans dare to return and provoke the Jews by organizing a new *"Akzion?"*

The Germans are no longer the master race. In their amazingly rapid victories the first breaches appear. Field-Marshal Paulus, who led a stubborn campaign against the Russians and reached the outskirts of Stalingrad, falls captive with hundreds of thousands of his soldiers. Stalingrad has not fallen, Leningrad has not been captured, Moscow remains outside the reach of the *Wehrmacht.* Into the closed and frozen Teutonic mind an uninvited factor, totally rejected and unacknowledged, steals in – fear.

The tireless efforts of the Jewish underground to acquire weapons bear fruit. There is no longer a fighter without his own personal weapon. This one has a revolver, the other a rifle, and the third, a dagger and a pair of grenades. And all this under the nose of the S.S. and the Gestapo, and the institutionalized, practiced and well-drilled German Army.

### Passover Eve, Nineteen Forty-Three

Monday, the eve of Passover, the nineteenth of April, nineteen forty-three. The Germans break into the Ghetto to capture Jews, and are greeted by well-aimed fire which kills some of them. Cries of despair escape from the mouths of the pure Aryans. Even S.S. units suffer significant losses, and retreat in panic.

The German command is surprised. S.S. General Jorgen Strup assembles his troops, reviews their ranks, tries to encourage them with routine words. His voice shakes.

The Germans try several times to send deputations to conduct negotiations on "very easy" terms, as they put it – but encounter bursts of gunfire.

According to the data supplied by Jorgen Strup himself, 1,262 soldiers and 31 officers were activated on the first day of the revolt. This number would swell in the following days. The Jews do a fine job in planning their operation and in improvising traps. Two out of three of the old mines in their possession are set off at the right place, the appropriate time and in the most effective manner, significantly increasing the German losses. The panic continues, and confusion characterizes the operations of the German officers, both senior and junior. The Jews have almost no losses. Their movements are calculated, every shot is well aimed. Ammunition is scarce, and must be saved.

An amazingly composed elderly man named Diamant, armed with an old, long-barreled rifle, sits in an attic, shooting from behind a small window. The fighters say he is "phlegmatic." After they watch him for half a day, they coin a new saying: "With Diamant, every bullet – a German!" The statement is true. Diamant is an easy-going person, who lives alone, and, like the decisive majority of his young friends, followers and admirers, he will not be counted among the few survivors.

## Zamenhof Street

Jacob Lipschitz takes part in the battle raging in Zamenhof Street. An S.S. unit penetrates the street from the western side, advances eastward in two columns while firing to intimidate, and reaches the corner of Zamenhof and Mila Streets. There it is greeted by heavy fire from grenades and firearms. The S.S. force retreats, and here a surprise awaits them: two groups of fighters, with Jacob Lipschitz in one of them, open well-aimed fire at them from the building entrances and from the street itself. The Germans suffer losses, lose control, run in panic and gather in the middle of the street, where they receive a rain of home-made incendiary bombs from the roofs and upper stories of the buildings. Desperate screams and calls for help in juicy S.S.-German, in shameful contrast to the declared ground rules for Aryan-German behavior. A few of the Germans succeed in escaping from the Zamenhof Street trap. The underground fighters descend to the fallen soldiers and take their weapons. Someone gives water to a dying German, another ignores him.

Once again, a truce deputation of three Germans – shaking with fear and carrying a white flag, unarmed except for the traditional bayonets in which they pride themselves. They ask a number of times for a cease-fire; they declare that they seek peace; they entreat the Jews to be so kind as to conduct negotiations. The answer is unequivocal: a liberating burst of gunfire.

## The Continuation

The concatenation of events is known. The battles continue hour after hour, day after day, night after night. The first, second and third weeks are more bitter, more daring, and, it seems, will never end. Tank and artillery fire destroys building after building, bunker after bunker. Airplanes, too, add their share to the malicious destruction. The Jews who are killed remain among their comrades, who still continue fighting. There is no place to remove them to. Their corpses rot. The Germans increase in number, and the Jews decrease. Even so, the Jews continue to surprise, raining down fire that decreases the enemy ranks, setting lethal traps for them, and appearing in the most unexpected places, while the Germans, still quite numerous, listen to every rustle, follow every movement tensely, at times surprising themselves and firing at each other, losing their grip.

## The End

The inevitable end: the Germans set fire to the Ghetto, or, more correctly, to what is left of it. The Ghetto goes up in flames, from one end to the other. No piece of stone, not one brick or door-frame remains which has not been burnt by the flammable materials at the Germans' disposal. The Jews left in the bunkers are baked in the hellish heat which dissolves everything, are choked by smoke, and, not infrequently, become human torches which fire at the enemy until the final collapse.

Those choked by smoke come out of their hiding places, where the *"Wehrmacht"* heroes await them. Those who have weapons shoot and are shot. Those who don't, surrender, and are tortured, murdered or sent to destruction.

According to the testimonies, for seven whole weeks the Germans have no rest in the destroyed Ghetto. From time to time, from the depths of the charred earth a shadow of a man rises, fires at the Germans, and flees. And if the bullets of the *Deutsche Soldaten* don't get him, and the Poles outside of the burning Ghetto don't betray him, his chances of surviving are good. From the third week on, the Ghetto looks like a huge cemetery, with fires raging in it, the air stifled by heavy screens of smoke. In the seventh week, the flames die down, but the smoke seems to increase, rising to unbelievable heights, spreading and dense. Everything is destroyed. And the Germans, it seems, have nothing left to do.

## Six by Six

Jacob Lipschitz was not killed, nor was he wounded. Fighters fell around him, and a whole family was buried in a neighboring bunker when a German soldier threw a grenade and an incendiary bomb into it. In the bunker where he had sat and fought for days and nights, Jacob Lipschitz was the only one left. And since his ammunition had run out, and he was unable to find a bullet anywhere, he threw his personal weapon, the "Parabellum," into a corner, like a worthless object. A great, alienating apathy descended upon him.

One evening, he sees himself crawl out to ground level. Ruins, as far as the eye can see. Clouds of thick smoke. There is no trace of the Ghetto. It is all over.

At his feet – hot ash, an ember which refuses to die, and the body of a killed S.S. officer. The German lies with his legs spread apart and a tormented look on his face. His jacket is open. The gray riding pants are held by a belt and suspenders. A curious swelling in the right shoulder pad draws his attention. He extends his hand, and from between the pliant strips of cloth he extracts a tiny revolver, completely new, about six centimeters by six centimeters. In the short barrel is a six point three five caliber bullet, ready for firing. And three more bullets in the short magazine. He has heard that S.S. officers keep such revolvers for times of distress, when they pretend to surrender to their enemy, pull the weapon out of their shoulder pads, shoot the soldier who is supposed to take them captive, and right after that, shoot themselves...

His palm closes on the revolver which has not yet been used. It totally disappears inside his hand.

Before he can straighten up, a familiar voice grates in his ear, commanding: "About face! Hands up!"

He complies with both commands, automatically.

Opposite him stands Fritz. The gleaming "Walther," with a newly fitted magazine, the safety off and a bullet in the barrel, is cocked in his outstretched hand.

The German smiles from ear to ear, ludicrously.

"The bullet meant for you is in the barrel!" he proclaims with coarse satisfaction, and sees fit to explain: "I've been watching you! I knew into which bunker you descended! I laid in wait for you. I showed forbearance!"

There is black soot on the Swabian farmer's gross, flushed face, especially on his nose, which Jacob for the first time notices is a pug-nose, like a button.

He didn't know who acted, or how, but in that split second he saw the tiny revolver in his own hand, which was strange to him, and felt his finger pull the trigger.

A stunning shot. The little revolver breaks into pieces. A spring, a screw and metal parts fly in all directions from the force of the blast. Well, all those stories about the S.S. officers who shoot their captors with such a revolver and then turn it around and shoot themselves are a lie. This tiny revolver cannot fire more than a single shot. A single six point three five caliber bullet.

Through the smoke, which has not ceased ascending to the sky, pillar after pillar, he sees how the German's mouth is wide open, his red maw bared in all its horrible depth, while the satisfied expression on his face changes beyond recognition before his eyes. The impervious assurance, the gross maliciousness, the dark satisfaction, make way for sudden panic, recoil and pain and, most of all: wonderment. Abysmal, unforeseen, childish wonderment. With evident effort, the Swabian pronounces, slowly, word after word:

"A Jew, and not a dirty Jew!" – and falls on his back, like a monument.

A great thud, raising a thick cloud of dust, which does not succeed in disturbing the terrible quiet which has descended on the scene of the shooting.

He skips over the fresh corpse without thinking about it. He ascends the heap of ruins, on which a number of corpses are scattered in a variety of strange positions. Smoke screens everything. His eyes are burning. He sits on what was once the railing of a balcony. His body needs rest. A body not his. He sits bent over, frozen, foreign to the world, and the world is foreign to him.

Nothing is left. No one is left. Only he. Where should he go? His question does not concern him. It was not he who asked it. It is not he who has to answer it.

He sat and continued sitting, without changing his position, without moving a limb. Hours upon hours. A day, maybe two days, maybe... he will never remember.

## Ivan Novotny

Jacob Lipschitz survived. He joined the Partisans, was recruited into the Red Army, reached Berlin, and deserted. At some point, after weary travels through destroyed Europe, he decided to study medicine. He had no papers. He had not completed high school. Then he heard a rumor about a Slovakian Jew, who had fought the Germans, survived, and returned to Bratislava, his birthplace. Slovaks who had collaborated with the Germans and had sent the relatives of this Jew, who was a high-school teacher by profession, to the extermination camps, were afraid that he would want to take revenge on them, and immediately appointed him Principal of the central high school in their city. And he, without batting an eyelid, had begun issuing legal matriculation certificates to any Jew who approached him, all signed in his own hand and sealed with the required seals. When asked why he did this, he answered that it was insignificant compensation for all that had been done to the Jews in this war.

Jacob Lipschitz traveled to Bratislava, found this Jew, asked for a matriculation certificate, and the latter gave it to him, leaving blank the spaces for given name, surname and date of birth. Jacob

Lipschitz wrote down his correct date of birth, and, in the place for "surname," wrote in a clear and sure manner, with the official black marker: "Novotny," a quite common Czech name. And in the place for "given name," he wrote "Ivan," which sounds more Russian and generally Slavic than Czech.

I met him in Prague, towards the end of 1946. Like myself, he studied medicine at Karl University. He lived at the ancient and prestigious student dormitory, the name of which was changed to Piatvo Kvietna, the Fifth of May, the day Prague was liberated by the Red Army. My friend B. was his roommate, and that was how we became acquainted. His strong, olive-tinted features, his frizzy hair, and his sad, dark eyes, made his origin evident at a distance. Notwithstanding, I asked him if he was a Jew. He smiled, a sad, forgiving smile, and answered in a dull voice that he was not a Jew and had no link or connection with that miserable people which, as he put it, had paid the heaviest price in the war that had just ended. In spite of my surprise, I could do nothing but accept the words of Ivan Novotny, and be satisfied with them.

As fate willed it, we both happened to meet at the spacious Turkish bath of that students' dormitory, the "Kolej", which, as stated earlier, was renowned. Now his claims were refuted. When we went up to the room, he, with no alternative, but not unwillingly, revealed his story to me. When he concluded it, he must have felt uneasy, and found it necessary to explain:

"To be born a Jew is a curse. I have no more strength to carry this burden. Nor have I the will."

He completed his studies and became a successful doctor in the United States of America.

## About the Author

Shlomo Kalo (1928-2014) was born in Sofia, Bulgaria. From the age of 12, was active in an anti-Fascist underground. At the age of 15, was arrested and exiled to a concentration camp. At the age of 18, won a prize in a poetry competition. Studied medicine in Prague where he also worked as a journalist. As an overseas volunteer for the newly established Israel he was sent to train as a pilot in Olomouc. Kalo immigrated to Israel in 1949. He was awarded M.Sc. in microbiology by the Tel-Aviv University and later became director of medical laboratories in Israel's largest health care service.

The sharp turn in his life which occurred in the first week of 1969 has been reflected ever since in his creation. 80 books of his were published in Israel: Literary fiction and literary non-fiction on a variety of themes, and in an amazing variety of genres. His books were published in 16 countries. During the last years of his life Shlomo Kalo was nominated for the Nobel Prize in Literature.

### Other titles by Shlomo Kalo:

*THE CHOSEN* An historical epic based on the Biblical story of Daniel.
*ATHAR* - A Holocaust memoir
*ERRAL* - An autobiographical novel
*LILI* - A novel
*THRILLER The Galilee Plot*
*THE TROUSERS – Parables for the 21st Century.*